strategies in
humanistic education

volume 3

tim timmermann

and

jim ballard

a mandala book

Library of Congress
Catalog Card Number
75-25394

ISBN   0-916250-25-3

Table of Contents

If you need to reproduce the materials in this book, please feel free to do so. As you make additions to the contents or if you have suggestions for future volumes we would like to know about them.

If you reproduce any of these materials please give credit by including the following statement:

Reproduced from . . .
Strategies in Humanistic Education, Volume 3
Tim Timmermann
and
Jim Ballard
Mandala Press
P.O. Box 796
Amherst, MA. 01002

This permission is granted only for reproduction for educational/training events. Permission is not given for large scale-reproduction for sales distribution. If you include a portion of these materials in another publication, please write to us for permission to do so.

Mandala Press is a publishing house dedicated to providing humanistic and transpersonal education approaches to educators, social service workers, nurses clergy, recreational directors, etc. By providing "New Age" approaches to the world environment we are seeking to contribute to a planet of peace, enlightenment and creativity. We invite you to submit articles, manuscripts, ideas and thoughts to expand our present product line.

If you are interested in receiving training in our approaches or sponsoring one of our workshops in your area please write for further information to:

MANDALA MINDSKILLS FOUNDATION
P.O. Box 511
Amherst, MA. 01002

Introduction

Volume III of Strategies in Humanistic Education represents our continuing effort to bring quality materials to educators who are committed to humanizing education.

We've maintained the format from Volume I and II, finding it useful and effective.

The first part of the book outlines "How To." In this section we describe four different strategies (how to's) in conducting humanistic education activities. Volume I covered the S-I-S-F model, brainstorming, circletime, discussion methods, journals, continuums, role-play, small-group methods, fantasy, processing, and the W.U.B. worksheet. Volume II covers the S-I-P-A Self Growth Plan, forced choice, rank-order, inventories, spectrum, support groups, and energizers. (Summaries of these strategies can be found in the appendix.) Volume III covers Phoney Words, Affirming Strategies, Kid-As-Teacher and Whips.

In the second section of this book "Activities" we have chosen eleven themes which incorporates human issues, desires, needs or concerns, such as "Being Well," "Feelings," "Beyond Self," "Where Opposites Connect."

One change which has occured in Volume III is that we have placed a greater emphasis on transpersonal education. As we explore and discover new alternatives to our own personal growth these will be reflected in our strategies series.

Philosophy

There is a strong philosophical system underlying our *Strategies* series, and it is presented here in outline form. Basically, the ideas in this book rest on the following broad assumptions:

- People are their own greatest resource; the seeds of growth and solutions lie inside, not outside, the grower/problem-solver.

- Awareness of self is essential to choosing responsibly.

- Each of us is responsible, and we are always choosing, in any situation, what to notice as having meaning, and thus how to respond.

- Fear is our major limiter.

- Alternatives for meeting needs can always be found or generated, then chosen.

- Being right does not always work.

The How-To Section

The How-To Section

Here is a list of skills and strategies that are included in this section:

- Kid as Teacher

- Whips

- Phoney Words

- Affirming Strategies

Refer to this section whenever needed, to conduct the activities in the Activity Section, which are keyed back to the items in this section. Vary the methods according to group needs, time limits, and your own intuition.

Kid-As-Teacher

Introduction

A learning environment often tends to be more dynamic and enjoyable when it includes opportunities for learners to be teachers, leaders or facilitators of an activity. The ancient "show-and-tell" activity stays around because it 'works' — that is, it continues to have perceivable payoff to both teachers and students. Teachers of reading sometimes report that there is more enjoyment and more seems to "get done" when kids are seated in pairs, taking turns reading aloud to each other. Committee work or games in which youngsters take the leader's part often spark more enthusiasm in the task. Allowing kids to be teachers can lift a burden off of teachers — the one that says "you're the teacher; therefore you are responsible for anything and everything that happens."

Schools have tended to make use of the kid-as-teacher (K-A-T) strategy either through informal, show-and-tell type activities, or through more formalized tasks such as debates, oral reports and speeches. In these traditional modes of having a student operate before the class, the emphasis is primarily on the "performer" role of the teacher. Seldom is the *facilitator* role shared with kids.

Letting kids be teachers may mean giving up (sharing) some of the power, authority, expertise and decision-making that the institution tends to place and keep solely in the hands of adults. Key here is what we refer to as one's *Give-Take Ratio*. Every teacher strikes, and tends to maintain, a certain ratio or balance, when interacting with a class, between giving (output) and taking (input), out of the 100% of the day's energy, time, talk, etc. For teachers this ratio is of crucial importance, for if you give mostly, you limit what kids can give to you or to each other. The K-A-T strategy is designed to help you to adjust your give-take ratio *back* — so that you are "taking" more, and students get to assume more of the responsibility for what is going on.

Thus, in lesson-planning, ask yourself the following:

Which activities, if any, lend themselves to student leadership?
What guidelines can I offer the K-A-T?
How will I support the K-A-T, without taking over?
How will leadership be shared (if not now, eventually) among students?

Experiment

One example of a good way to introduce the *concept* of Kid-As-Teacher is the following:

Each-One-Teach-One: Tell students they are each to plan or bring something — some skill or knowledge — to school and spend 10 minutes teaching someone else. *Guidelines:*

1. Choose something specially known to you — you know how to do it well, or all about it; and you think most other people don't.

2. Choose something that can be taught in ten minutes.

3. It can be useful, or merely fun.

4. Be non-competitive, and come prepared to learn from someone else.

The next day, have them choose partners and spend 20 minutes in teaching-learning diads. Process: How did it feel to "be the teacher?"

Often, breaking the class into small groups (3 to 8) is the way to employ K-A-T. This might be only for a small portion (5-10 minutes) of the period or day; perhaps as a kickoff (choosing a topic, developing concensus, preparing an agenda, etc.) of a follow-up (processing the activity just completed, giving feedback, drawing conclusions, evaluating, etc.). In each group, a leader-facilitator is appointed to 'run' the group.

As for total-class experiences, you will be surprised, once you begin to look for them, how many opportunities there are for you to share the teacher role with a child, simply by briefly 'priming' her or him, (i.e., telling an answer or solution, or sharing a process) and letting the kid do precisely what you would have done. (Be aware of your own ownership needs here; often it is the very things you enjoy *most* about teaching that lend themselves best to the K-A-T strategy!)

Many — perhaps most — of the activities in this *Strategies* series are suitable for K-A-T, once you have modeled the leader role in them and clarified roles and guidelines through prior experiencing. These activities include Circletime, leading open-ended discussions (K-A-T simply calls on and acknowledges contributors), guided fantasy, games, brainstorming, small-groups, energizers, and many of the out-loud processing techniques (see Vols. I and II of *Strategies In Humanistic Education.*)

There is no point in making K-A-T an exercise in embarassment. To smooth the role transmission, here are

Some Suggestions

1. The first few times you do a K-A-T, *choose the teacher yourself*. It should be a person who a) basically seems to accept him/herself; b) is somewhat comfortable in this sort of role, okay with the spotlight; and c) has high trust and acceptance by the class or group. (This suggests that your "ham" may not be the best to start with, for she or he may use the stage to create a "though act to follow.") Mostly, you're after a *success* this first time, and a feeling in other kids of "*I* could do that!"

2. Choose the task yourself. Make it one whose design allows easy, minimal direction, and which is short and fairly fast-paced.

3. Be ready to support the K-A-T, stepping in as a consultant only if asked for or obviously needed.

4. Maintain tight time limits. Cut off the activity before or as enthusiasm peaks.

5. Make sure the K-A-T role gets passed around. Volunteers, names in a hat, working through the class list, alternating boys and girls — all are alternatives after a successful beginning.

6. Keep asking yourself, with continued successes using K-A-T: "What else could I give away?"

Whips

A whip is a sentence with a blank in it.

    I really like _____ .

    My favorite TV program is _____ .

    When I'm alone I wish _____ .

A whip is appropriate as an opener or to close a session with a group. The effect of a whip is social ease, sharing a sense of being part of a whole.

Start by saying the sentence and filling in the blank as a model for the group. Start anywhere in the group. Each person gets a chance in turn to respond, each having the "pass" option. Tasks may be related to issues in the group, subject matter, or chosen totally at random.

Examples of Whips:

    A favorite _____ is _____ .

    I'm bothered when _____ .

    A hobby of mine _____ .

    When I'm new in a group I usually _____ .

    I wonder _____ .

    I wish _____ .

    I want _____ .

    I appreciate _____ .

    I'd like to be _____ .

    I'd be sad if _____ .

Whips can be used to process an activity or session:

    I felt _____ doing this.

I learned _____ .

I was pleased with _____ .

I am puzzled about _____ .

I like it when _____ .

I hope next time _____ .

If I could replan this session _____ .

I saw people _____ .

This group needs _____ .

What I like about this group _____ .

When the whips have been completed the people in the group can listen to each other by; saying things like:

You liked _____ .

You thought _____ .

Or have the people in the group share I-statements like:

I noticed _____ .

I saw _____ .

I heard _____ .

I got the sense that _____ .

I realized that _____ .

I became aware of _____ .

Whips are easy to use sharing opportunities which can be events for listening to each other and build community.

A favorite _(anything)_ is _____ .

Phoney Words

What you hear is what you want to hear and what you hear may not be what is said. As two people communicate there is the sender and receiver, the coder and decoder. The responsibility for what a person hears and decodes rests within that person. The responsibility for clarity and "straight" coding rests within the speaker.

Since both things are going on simultaneously (coding and decoding), the speaking/listening process can get complicated.

The purpose of this section is:

> to point out how some people code their words and don't say what they mean

> to give directions on how the decoder can "break-through" the coding garble

> to share activities for practicing "straight" coding in speech

There are some popular "cliche" type phrases that have been adopted in our speech. Some of them are:

> "It's hot in here."

> "This is hard work."

> "Will this ever stop?"

> "The boss is in a bad mood."

> "Money doesn't go as far."

What the person is usually saying behind the code is something about him/herself. There is either an unawareness feelings or an unwillingness to own up to some scary feelings, so that the person decides to say things in a non-first-person way.

The sentences above can be changed to:

"I'm hot."

"I'm tired."

"I want this to stop."

"I'm afraid of the boss today."

"I don't know how to manage my money."

By changing the words — it's, this, that, money, etc. to I or I'm — ownership is taken, blame is gone. The speaker now begins to take responsibility for his or her own feelings. The decoder has no problem understanding.

Another word for which there can be a substitute is the word "BUT." What usually happens with "but" is that it discounts the previous words.

Example:

"I like your hair-do, but....."

"Your golf swing has improved, but....."

"The paper you handed in is improved, but....."

The decoder will usually not remember or hear the first complimentary words. S/he will focus more on what comes after "but."

The substitute for "but" is "and." "And" naturally carries the listener along to the next thought or phrase. There is no negative with "and."

The third category of phoney words is the word "because." "Because" implies a cause that may be external to the speaker. If the person is using "because" to own a feeling or to explain how s/he did something, the blame factor is absent. If s/he is saying "It happened because he didn't . . . . . ," the blame factor is present.

"Because" is an illusion since no one can "do it" to anyone else.

Asking questions is another way of causing confusion in the coding/decoding process. Making statements is usually the clearer way of saying what's on one's mind and of making contact with another person. Almost all questions are really statements.

Examples:

Question	Statement
Why did you do that?	I don't understand what you did.
Is this OK?	I want your approval on this.
How many did you order?	I need more information about the order.
When are you going to the store?	I want you to go to the store.
Where did you buy that?	I like your outfit.

Making a statement forces the person to commit him/herself to express a feeling or describe a want. Intimacy is more possible, and tentativeness or uncertainty are diminished.

"If only" is a way of futuring or pasting instead of presenting. Presenting is living in the "NOW." It is believing "what is — is." There is no way to change past or future and "if only" deludes one into thinking or behaving that there is.

"They" is a way not to own one's own choosing. We make the assumption that no one can "do it" to another person without that person's conscious or unconscious cooperation.

> They did it to me again.

> They always behave that way.

> They can never be counted on.

"Can't" is a game word. It indicates the speaker is playing the "I'm not responsible for my actions" game. The speaker has not taken responsibility for the choice s/he has made. The two words which fit are "won't" or "don't."

If you hear a student saying "I can't skip rope," a clearer and truer statement might be "I don't skip rope." "I can't do this math" might mean "I won't do this math.

Sometimes "try" becomes the response to "can't." "Try" is amother game-inducing word. Like "lazy," "impudent," "proud" it is not a *doing* word but an attitude. Most people define it as an action of arousing energy to do something. What ultimately happens in the "trying" process is that the person either does something or doesn't do something. "Trying" can easily become a cop-out experience.

Affirming Strategies

Here are some ideas for the no-problem area that can be implemented right away in your classroom or school. Each is designed to give feedback to a person so that he or she:

- will feel noticed and worthwhile

- will gain self-awareness as a competent person

- will gain understanding of the process of affirmation, and want to use it with others

1. **Deserved Positive Feedback (DPF)** This is one of the easiest, and yet most potentially powerful of all. Its potential is virtually unexplored. Like Active Listening, it can be growth-producing in that it feeds back responsibility and reality to the other, making them feel understood and appreciated. It might be called "Active Noticing."

   There are at least three kinds of praise.

   a. *Evaluative* ("You are smart, beautiful, strong, etc.") This kind of feedback often feels good, but is confrontive, causes embarrassment. Liabilities are:

   - it's a You-Message, and likely will not be heard as intended

   - it makes the sender a judge

   - it may cause dependency, or a tendency to try to live up to the label

   - it may cause resentment, probably well-concealed (i.e. "You don't know about the times I fail")

   - it may hurt the relationship (pedestals are uncomfortable, shaky places) by causing embarrassment or weakening trust

20

b. *Descriptive* ("You did that" is the base phrase) . . . "You people lined up before coming in the room" . . . "You did five examples, Jerry" . . . "This class is working quietly" . . . "In this story, Marge, you first told the reader about the setting, then introduced the characters, then told what happened" . . . etc.

This kind of feedback is factual (deserved); conveys good feelings of appreciation (positive). It says: "I care about what you did, enough to notice it and tell you you did it." It does not run so much risk of embarrassment as a. above (i.e., difference between "You are gorgeous!" and "You wore really sunny colors today.")

c. *Appreciative* ("I like" or "I appreciate") This kind of feedback conveys positive emotion, and of course has all of the greater chance of being heard and internalized that any I-Message has, over a You-Message such as example a. above. Teachers can use a great deal of this at appropriate times:

"I appreciate your getting ready so fast."
"I like this part of your picture."
"I feel good about the way you helped me solve the problem of distributing scissors in a safe way."

DPF, then, is done using the models of descriptive or appreciative praise as defined above.

Instead of	Say	Or
Wow! This is the best class I've ever had!	"This class works well without my direction."	"I really like the way this class works."
"You're a super athlete."	"You ran the hundred in 21.2 seconds!"	"I'm proud of your time."
"You are really popular."	"I notice lots of kids ask to eat lunch with you."	"It pleases me to see how other kids respond to you."

Here are ways to use this in the classroom:

1. Quickie method: "Take a minute and look at the person on your right, and the person on your left. Now, take the sentence-stub 'I notice your . . ." or "Something I notice about you is . . ." and *tell* each other.

   Right away, the room changes. When I ask what happened, people say, "It felt good," "It was fun," "It's nice to be noticed."

2. *More focus* on DPF. Divide group into groups of 12 to 15, seated in circles. Have available, or have groups manufacture, enough torn pieces of paper for one each. To tear papers, crease 8 ½ x 11 plain paper carefully and exactly into eighths, then tear very carefully along lines and distribute. Eliminate pieces with obvious defects or tears or differences, so discrimination is more critical. Distribute pieces with directions not to change them in any way.

   Develop a model on board, with group's help, or *mental sentences*, entitled TASK/SELF sentences. Explain that in public-display-task situations, such as proliferate in schools and workshops and graduate classes, SELF is on the line. The big issues are: "Is this safe?" "Will I succeed?" "Will I look tall or small?" Now, say "In a few minutes, I'm going to ask you to put all the papers in the center of your circle, and then *find yours.*" Anxiety level rises in group, evidenced by noisy reaction and immediate perusal of paper pieces by members. Develop, thru discussion with group about what's going on on a feeling level, following sentences on board:

   a. I want to do it (right, well, the way the teacher says)
   b. I think I can/can't do it (right, well, etc.)
   c. I do what I can to make sure I do it (right, etc.)

Now, direct group to find partners in the circle, and tell each other about their pieces and their distinguishing characteristics. It's get-to-know-your-piece-of-paper-time. Allow 3-5 minutes. Direct active-listening reponses, as partners tell each other back, "Your piece of paper has . . ." Stop, place papers in center of circle. Add sentence on board:

d.   I try the task . . .

and direct participants to "As you now *find your papers*, try also to notice what your partner does."

Allow time to sort out papers, discuss, and work through any difficulties (occasionally, someone is convinced "someone took my paper" and must walk around with the paper they found left over and compare it with others until everyone is satisfied).

Ask group to raise hands, "How many of you found your piece of paper?" Add sentence to board:

e.   I do the task.

Now say, "I'm going to ask you to do a couple of obvious things. First, did you find your paper? (nods) Then tell yourself, inside, 'I found my piece of paper.' " "Secondly, did your partner find his/her paper? (nods) I want you to *tell* your partner what he/she did." (Laughs. "You found your piece of paper.") Add sentence to board:

f.   You did the task. (Circle 6 and 7 and label "Intervention by other.")

Ask: "*Can* your partner find his/her paper?" (nods) "How do you know?" (Answer: "Because he/she just did it!") "*Tell* your partner that he/she can." Add sentence to board:

g.   You can do the task.

Say, "Can *you* find your piece of paper?" (Yes) "How do you know?" (I just did.) "Tell yourself silently that you *can* do this task." Add sentence:

h.   I can do the task.

Note to teachers:

Suggest that I-Canness is something teachers want to build into kids. There's a lot of I-Can'tness around in schools. Issue is, how do I build -canness into kids? Refer to sentences on board, and label sentences 1-6 DOING sentences, and sentences 7-8 BEING sentences. "Humans get DOING and BEING all mixed up." We use a 3-stage self-processing process to gain ideas about ourselves:

1.   choose
2.   act
3.   reflect on the outcome of our action

Each of these reflections give us a "self-percept," thousands of which help us form a "self-concept." But it helps if SOMEONE ELSE outside of us tells us what we did, gives us help in step-3 above.

THE POINT IS: "We can help build i-can-ness into kids (or, more accurately, help *them* build i-can-ness into themselves, by *telling them what they did*, after they do it."

When do we usually, as teachers, tell kids "You can do it!" (Answer: *before* they do something, to get them to do it.) Often, we know and they know that that's a manipulation-type encouragement.How about *waiting* until they've done something, and *then* telling them "You did it. You can do it."

Workshop or classroom assignment: *Tell someone what they did* that was neutral-to-positive; give DPF in a real-life situation.

Anecdote from a teacher-friend: I was giving a third grade spelling practice test. A boy Tom, sitting next to where I was standing, had never written *any*thing for me, all year, nor had he former years. I gave the word "spell" and decided to give a lot of help. I said "Who can tell me the first sound of 'spell'?" ("Sssss") "Okay, write the 'Sssss'-sound on your paper." I looked down, and Tom had written an S. I said to him privately, "Tom, you wrote the Ssss-sound." "Now, what's the next sound in 'spell'?" ("Puh") "Okay, write the puh-sound after the sss-sound." I looked, and Tom had written a P. I told him, "Tom, you wrote the puh-sound." It went on like that until he'd written the word "spell." I said to him, "Tom, you wrote the word, 'spell.' You can write a word." From then on, he wrote every word, and even came and asked me what the other words were before 'spell,' so he could write those too, and catch up. Tom became a writer in our class. And I was careful always to feed back what he'd done, tell him what he *could* do *after* he'd done it.

2. **Apprecio-grams**. Teachers can direct kids to write "ap-precio-grams" to each other and distribute them during a given day. These are also nice at faculty level, to be left in teacher's boxes.

3. **Cheap A's.** Often, the grade of A must be so striven for and is so elusive that many kids turn off on working for grades, while others make it their whole reason-for-being at school. Figure out what deserves an "appreciative A" in your classroom, and use all those extra empty pages of your roll-book to put down high grades for the behavior you appreciate. Examples:

"A" for being considerate of someone
"A" for bringing a pencil
"A" for being in your seat
"A" for helping
"A" for coming to class on time

Testimonial: "As a junior-high teacher, I used to have a lot of trouble about the issue of pencils. I'd assign something, and suddenly I'd hear 'I can't do it 'cause I don't have a pencil.' One day I told the class, 'Whoever has a pencil here today gets an "A" in my book' — and I took a show of hands and wrote "A's" down in one of the rollbook empty pages. I kept it up for several days. Before long, my room was filled with pencils." Here, "A's" for pencil-bringing solved a problem. It's a type of behavior-modification, but the controls lie inside the kid, not the teacher, and the "A" is a way of saying "I appreciate your effort." (Caution: Never use one of these methods as a club. In other words, don't start calling attention to negative behavior, by saying "watch out, or you won't get your 'A'." Another teacher told me: she had a mother say in confidence, "James's 'A' for being on time in your class is the first 'A' he's ever had in school, and he came right home and told us about it." One wonders: three small lines on a piece of paper — A — how important it is! to kids, and to teachers in a graduate class! How can a teacher turn all that energy into legitimately rewarding, without placing total emphasis on evaluation, which is, in the end, what all this A-business is about?

4. **Apple for the Teacher.** Try putting apples in every teacher's box at your school. See what happens.

5. **Secret Pal Day** (can work at student *or* faculty level) Tell group a day or week ahead that such-and-such-a-date is "Secret Pal Day." On S-P-D, names of all group (class) members are placed in a hat and picked. The task for each member (student) is to think of something to do for the person picked, that will make that person feel good, special, appreciated. Gifts or messages can be left on desks, in boxes, or transmitted through middle-persons. The choice is the teacher's, administrator's, or group's, as to whether or not to reveal "secret pals" at the end of the day or period of time allotted.

26

6. **Certificates.** If given as legitimate, caring means of showing appreciation — not as "carrots" held out to be earned or worked-for — certificates are an easy way to give kids Deserved Positive Feedback. (After all, why are pictures of you, remarks by peers, and your "Most Likely To . . ." in your old high school yearbook among the most important items in that volume to you? Every person is, after all, his/her own World's Most Important Person.)

A sixth-grade teacher reported: "In our school we always have Awards Day, on which a certain elite number of kids received semi-engraved parchment certificates of achievement or faculty approval. Everyone looked forward to it, but there were always only a limited number of 'winners.' I decided to put my own version of a certificate on a ditto master. I used a ruler and ballpoint, making fake-french-lace border and fake-old-english heading, ran off a hundred or so and put the stack in my desk drawer. The whole operation probably cost me a half-hour of work, and boy, did it pay off! At the end of each day, I'd fill out two or three of those, and give them out, for whatever it was I felt appreciation for that day. I kept records, and made sure every kid got one in the course of a month or so. The kids and I looked forward to 'certificate time.' An one father told me: 'my daughter has hers framed, under glass, in her bedroom. It's getting a little dim, but it meant so much to her!' " Here's one format:

This is to certify that _____

has successfully completed requirements for this

special award in the field of _____ .

Date _____ Room _____ Teacher _____

Certificates can be given for the same areas as Item 3 above. The more specific, the better. (i.e. " . . . in the field of

being nice to himself _____

27

7. **Feed-back to Bernie Day.** Choose a boy or girl in your class and write his/her name in your lesson plan book as a "target for feedback" for that given day. Give Deserved Positive Feedback (either the "you did" or "I like" models, or combinations). The next day, pick another student for your "active noticing," and so on.

The *major issue* in using any Affirming Strategy is: How can I give a child feedback on what I notice him or her doing that is positive, caring of self or other, constructive, or otherwise deserving of my appreciation. And: how can I do that in such a way that it enhances self-esteem, creates independency rather than dependency, and feeds into a classroom climate of "I-count-you-count?"

Obviously, there are many other devices for affirming, for building self-esteem, and for training in effective communication. They all come under the heading of Affirming Strategies, in the same way that other systems use strokes (Transactional Analysis), or Strength Bombardment (NTL and others). Teachers really can never do too much of this.

The Activity Section

Being Well

Introduction

Suppose that at any given moment you and I have exactly the state of physical, mental, and emotional health and well-being we *choose*. ("Choose" here may mean: (1) deliberately and consciously select; (2) buy into, hiding the fact of choice from ourselves by representing germs, foods, doctors, epidemics, medications and other "outside agents" as determiners of ourselves; (3) recognize as a portion of our script, or what "happens to people like us"; or (4) settle for, by not seeing and appropriating other options.)

The "new" field of holistic medicine assumes that the *self* is the ultimate healer, teacher, helper and knower, and that it is to the resource of our own minds that we must turn in order to "live well." Health and well-being, holism asserts, are *normal* states; thus, disease, infirmity and dependency are aberrations that need not be tolerated. The holistic mentality challenges widespread root assumptions about our own limitations. Thus, it is with our personal belief systems that we and our students must struggle in appropriating holism's assertions regarding our innate potency. A holistically oriented unit of study like this one affords students glimpses of themselves that are seldom reflected from a media that pushes pills, a medical profession whose model of health focuses on disease, or a society that sees stress as normal and reliance on experts as a fact of life.

Your own awareness, as teacher, of how your own personal belief systems impinge on your state of health is, of course, key to your success in implementing this unit. Each of the exercises should be practiced and experienced by you, before you present it to your students.

Purposes

- To strengthen each student's trust and confidence in his/her own organism

- To normalize health, happiness and well-being

- To dispel awe of dis-ease and redefine it as an *act* or *attitude* of the self (i.e. something I've "bought")

- To create awareness and assertiveness on the part of students as consumers to medical services

- To teach practical and preventive ways of self-healing

- To confront each student with the following assumptions, and to cause each to interact creatively with them:

    1. No one causes you to believe what you believe, or to think in any particular manner . . .

    2. The concept of fault or blame has no relevance with regard to what you or I "buy" as being what-is-so . . .

    3. Beliefs *precede* experience, and can be changed if experience is "negative" (not working) for the person.

Definition

Have each student write (or dictate to you) at least 3 endings
for each . . .

Health . . .

Sickness . . .

Doctors . . .

Medicine . . .

Hospitals . . .

When I feel bad . . .

My body . . .

Collate the answers onto a ditto'd handout. Use the lists as
discussion-starters: "What samenesses do you pick up? How
do we seem to feel about these issues? Can our conclusions
be put together into single "group" endings for each item?"

Discussion Starters

- Which is normal, sickness or health? Say more about your answer.

- When you are well, who makes (keeps) you that way? When you are sick, who makes you that way? When you get well again, who makes you that way?

  > (Reflect answers by paraphrasing, making no attempt to "steer" the discussion. Afterwards, ask for sum-ups of attitudes.)

- Each day, place a new statement from below in a prominent place, and discuss it the *following* day:

  — You're only as sick as you think.

  — The body heals itself, sometimes using help.

  — If you think you need glasses to see, you do.

  — If you think you can't . . . you *can't*.

  — You select your sickness.

  — We already know how to heal ourselves.

  — We've already healed ourselves.

- How come, if there are deadly germs inside of us all the time, we don't die or get sick all the time? How come that it changes, on occasion, and we become ill?

- What's an "expert"? How come some doctors get sick, dentists have toothaches, marriage counselors divorce, and psychiatrists kill themselves?

Circletime

- What it's like when I'm sick

- A time I know I decided to get sick

- On a scale of totally-helpess (zero) to totally-in-charge (ten) . . . How I feel about staying healthy (and why)

- A time I healed myself

- A time I felt myself getting sick, and just decided I *wouldn't* . . . and didn't

- How I feel about doctors (pills, shots, hospitals, dentists, counselors, psychologists)

- How TV affects the way I feel about the being-well/sick issue

- My 3 deepest beliefs about my own body's health

- A person whose general state of health I have feelings about

- A worry about my health

- A dream, wish, or fantasy I have about getting sick or dying

- Who or what influences me most in the being sick/well issue

Journals

Influences

- I get my notions about health and disease mostly from (rank-order):

    ___ parents

    ___ friends

    ___ teachers

    ___ watching TV (what? _____)

    ___ dreams

    ___ my body

    ___ doctors

    ___ things I've read (what? _____)

    ___ other (?) _____

Health Log

- Keep a Journal record of your state of health for 30 days, using a scale of 0 (totally ill — about to die!) to 10 (*hugely* healthy and energetic!) Make a number-note here at ___time___ each day. What things do you notice, from keeping this log?

Planning How to Feel

- In the space below, write yourself a letter (using only sentences that begin "I will . . . .") about how you plan to feel tomorrow. Look back at the letter at least two other times today. Check tomorrow.

Being Well

- Decide, by yourself, on a goal of yours related to being healthier (you may think of "stopping" something, but that's often hard. . . . Think of *starting* something, instead — some new, easy thing, but something you're not presently doing. Note it below, as an "I will . . .")

  Don't tell anyone you are starting this — just do it.

Looking at my Beliefs

- Make a list of at least five things — areas, events, relationships, habits, attitudes, repeated happenings, patterns, etc. — that are *negative* for you.

  Example: "I never seem to make friends easily." (This is only negative if you *want* to make friends, and can't seem to.)

  Now next to each "negative," begin to list your *beliefs* — statements that say what you feel is so, for you, in that area. Keep "digging under" each one, to find the belief — the thing you've "bought into" — that *supports* that other belief. *Example:*

Negative	Beliefs
I never seem to make friends easily.	People aren't attracted to me.
	People don't like me.
	I'm not likeable.
	I don't deserve to be liked.
	I'm bad.

(*Teacher*: Here it is: the almost-always answer to un-health of any sort — the deeply-held belief that "I am unworthy." Self-concept is at the root of physical, as well as all aspects of personal (and even societal) well-being or unwell-being. Recognition of this fact can help *you* to be a more effective "helping agent" in your interacting generally with others. It means that you're a good teacher (in fact) — or a "bad" teacher — if you *believe* you are. What *are* we telling ourselves, at root?

This fact also helps to explain what healing is all about, and what the "healing agent" does, if s/he is effective. All healers who are effective — whether they are medical doctors, nurses, friends, faith-healers, lovers, teachers, witch-doctors, surgeons, or medicine-men — know that *the patient's beliefs about her/himself are the key to the healing process.* The healer thus works to get the patient to change these, and thus to "get well." This is not to say that sickness does not exists; it does. The person who is sick *is* sick. Her/his body has lowered its resistance, somehow, in *response* to what s/he has bought, at root, about him/herself! If this belief is "un-bought," the body responds, by upping its resistance, and "getting well." Obviously, most often the patient is not *aware* of the immobilizing power of this belief. But s/he can find the belief with direction. Beliefs are always conscious.

Roleplay

Doctor and Patient

Scene One: Patient comes to see Doctor, complaining s/he "can't sleep at night." After an examination, Doctor declares nothing wrong. Patient goes away, shaking head, obviously unsatisfied.

Scene Two: Patient returns, complaining s/he still can't sleep, acting desperate. Scene goes just as before.

Scene Three: Patient, now frantic ("You've *got* to do something!"), returns. Doctor goes aside, talks to self: "Guess I better try the old water-pill trick . . ." (turns to Patient) "Here, these should do the trick. Take two every night before you go to bed. You'll sleep like a baby." Patient: "Thanks, Doc! Thanks!" (obviously believing they'll do the trick.)

Scene Four: Patient takes pills, lays down, falls asleep immediately.

Aside: Doctor looks nonplussed: "How do I get her/him off the pills?"

Discussion: What are some possible titles for this skit? (Brainstorm.) Who healed the patient? Who heals anybody? How do beliefs affect healing?

(An alternate version, which could be used with a different ailment, would have *two* patients, coming at separate times, getting the same advice. Patient #1 is the "doubter" ("These pills won't work!"), while Patient #2 believes. Patient #1 remains sleepless (or with headaches, stomach aches, rash, coughs, etc.) while Patient #2 recovers.

Being Well

Activities

☆

Complaints

Count the number of *complaints* you hear, in a single 24-hour period, that in any way relate to the complainer's *health*. Do the same for positive statements, and compare. Is it more "fashionable" to do one than the other?

☆

Seeing Better

Dr. Herbert W. Bates, a noted opthalmologist, explains that vision is a *mental* phenomenon, and that impaired vision is always due to strain, good vision always due to concentrated relaxation. There are at least two ways of utilizing the list of relaxation exercises below. The first (A) is more like practice, and the second (B) more like an experiment (which often has startlingly successful results). (B acts as an excellent lead-in to A.)

A. Sequential practice: Instruct the class in each of the following exercises as a group over several different brief sessions, and encourage them to practice individually to improve vision.

B. Pre- and Post-Test:

  1. *Pretest.* Have children reseat themselves to work together in pairs. Give each pair a 6 foot length of string.

  2. Have all students with glasses or contact lenses remove them — and do the same yourself if you wear corrective lenses.

c. *Central Fixation.* People with normal vision "see best where they are looking" — that is, it can be demonstrated that they do not see as well objects to the slight periphery of the gaze-point. To practice this (and induce relaxation, hence better vision), have everyone choose an object to look at — such as a large letter — at some distance. Look at, for example, a T, at the right-most endpoint of the character or object. Then, switch to looking at the left-most point, and call to your own attention that you now see the rightmost point *worse* than before, when you looked directly at it. Switch back, and call to your own attention (attending is key) that you now see the *left* point worse. Repeat this "switching" several times. Practice making the distance smaller or shorter (at which you notice the point-not-observed-worse) if you can, by choosing a shorter span of the same object (say, the distance through the arm of the T, using corners now), if possible.

   Repeat palming.

d. Now, set up the pair-work again. Have the former distances re-measured or re-established, to determine whether some students can now see the formerly out-of-range letter or word.

(*Note:* Because this type of activity is such an individual experience, be ready to adopt a "no-big-deal" attitude. Remember that not only is it an exercise in relaxation of eye muscles, but of belief systems as well. Some students (particularly those who wear corrective lenses) may not be able to "let go" of their belief in their own inability to see well long enough to experience the benefits of the activity — or, they may even deny the results of the experiment and "hang on" to their belief

3.   Have one person in each pair hold a book, card, or
     other printed matter as near or far away as is ap-
     propriate in order to measure the distance (using the
     string, and marking it) exactly at what point they can
     not distinguish a certain letter or word (i.e., it is just
     outside of visual range). Have partners measure or
     mark this point, and repeat process for the other in
     each pair.

4.   *Practice.* Now, students work on their own, following
     your directions:

     a.   *Palming.* For about a minute or so, place hands
          over eyes, fingers crossed over forehead, and
          attempt to see utter blackness. The seeing of
          complete black indicates complete *relaxation* of
          the eye muscles; the seeing of grey, lights,
          shapes, etc. is, according to Dr. Bates, a
          completely mental phenomenon, and can be
          "practiced away" by imagining:

                one, or a series of black objects (cat, hat,
                space, well bottom, cave, etc.)

                imagining a black dot growing larger.

                imagining an object associated with
                pleasant feelings, then returning attention
                to one of the above.

     b.   *Swinging.* Stand with the feet about one foot
          apart, hands on hips, and swing through a 180°
          arc, from side to side, lifting the opposite heel
          each time. Do not try to conc ntrate on
          anything, but *look at it all* as it goes by, without
          straining. Do this 50 times. Sit down and do
          another minute of palming.

enough to convince themselves they can't see better when they *can*. Be ready for any and all results. Don't push anyone to participate, and don't push for any particular results. Do, however, follow up with processing, on an "I-level.")

☆

Interviewing

Have committees of 2 or 3 students conduct short interviews with doctors, dentists, psychologists, lawyers, nurses or counselors (or ask them to visit the class), asking the following questions:

1.   Do you believe people could be taught to do *without* the services of people of your profession? (If not totally, how much?)

2.   How much working time, out of 100%, do you spend on *preventing* disease, as against treating it?

3.   How much time, out of 100%, do you spend teaching the patient to heal him/herself?

4.   What is most exciting and energizing for you about doing the work you do?

5.   Exactly how do you decide how much (what fees) to charge?

6.   How do you think your profession is changing, if it is? How do you feel about these changes?

7.   What 3 recommendations would you make to a young person just getting started in your profession?

☆

Healing Meditation

Practice this together in class.

Sit quietly and close your eyes. Relax. Focus attention on your breathing. Repeat the sound 'OM'' in your mind, and think of it as a sound that goes out internally, from a central point of your consciousness, to all of your body cells. Think of each of the millions of them — the bone and blood and nerve and skin and muscle and brain cells — as *hearing* the repeated healing sound of OM. There is no magic. Your own relaxed concentration is what "makes you whole." Spread the sound out ("O", as a song, on the inbreath, "M" as a humming, on the out).

Do this whenever you think of it. At stressful moments, it's particularly helpful.

☆

Accupressure

For headache or backache, spend a minute or two, several times in succession gently massaging the one hand with the other thumb and forefinger — at the soft area between where the thumb and forefinger bones meet.

Have students remove shoes and socks and give themselves a foot massage, experimenting by checking with the Japanese "shiatsu" accupressure diagram on the next page. (You can project this or photocopy it as a handout.) Each reflex point connects with the areas of the body designated. Ask students to massage firmly but gently with fingertips, using a rotating clockwise motion.

Sinuses · pituitary gland · Sinuses

back of neck · cervical region · back of neck

Eyes · Thyroid · Thyroid · Eyes

Ears · Lungs · Lung · Ears

Shoulder · Solar plexus · Stomach · Solar plexus · Shoulder

Liver · Pancreas · Pancreas · Heart

gall bladder · adrenal · spleen

Kidney · Kidney

transverse colon · Spine · Spine · tranverse colon

ascending colon · ureter · descending colon

small intestine) · small intestines)

bladder

joint · Sex · coccyx · Sigmoid

sciatic nerve · sciatic nerve · hip

bones & formation · bones & formation · thigh · knee

Right foot · Left foot

45

☆

Preventive Breathing

Start each day by lying on your back, arms comfortably at the sides, and knees raised, feet flat on floor. Relax. Each intake breath *raises* stomach; outbreath, *lowers* stomach in a rolling motion. Two minutes of this could well prevent colds and other diseases.

To the Teacher:

As mentioned, one's *beliefs* about one's health are determiners of it. (This is not any different, really, from any other arena of experience:

> If you believe a person is lovable, s/he is!
> If you believe you are a bad person, facts are not important — you *act-as-if*.
> If you believe you can learn to do something you want to do, you will.)

Experience follows belief, not the other way around. This point cannot be emphasized too strongly.

If children react with statements like:

> "This is dumb! We're only *making-believe!*"

Say: "When are we *not* making believe?"

(Conduct a brainstorm of all the beliefs engaged at the present moment — everything from "these chairs will continue to hold us up" ... to ... "We're only making belief" (a belief). "*All* of our experience is based on our belief."

If children say:

> "I can't just change my beliefs around!"

Say:
"If you 'can't' (believe you can't) of course you 'can't' (won't) . . .
but it may be easier to think about changing your acting-as-if.
Notice that we're *acting as if* these chairs will hold us up.
That's the part we can change, in order to 'un-buy' one thing,
and buy into another."

(These kinds of responses on the learning-facilitator's part are
critical — they effectively turn the resistance back on the
resistor, in order to see that the resistance *itself* is based on a
contrary belief. Use at-hand situations, like the chairs, to
illustrate — and help students be aware — that "we are always
acting-as-if.")

A dynamic experiment, conducted in class with a warm, off-
hand manner, is the following (adapted from the humorous
"blue feather" example in Richard Bach's excellent book
Illusions):

☆

Imaging and Materializing an Object

Instruct students to sit quietly, close their eyes, and relax
(. . . = 3-second pauses) . . . "Let go of people and things
around you . . . your imagination, concentrate on a field of
beautiful, inky black velvet in front of you . . . now, let yourself
know that in a few moments — not yet — when I'm through
talking, you'll begin to see an object form, in front of your inner
eyes, against that black velvet background . . . Now, I want this
to be, for you, an *unusual* object, small enough to fit into your
hands . . . and I want you to just let it form itself, and even to
let yourself be surprised, if you are, at what it is . . . remember,
this should be something you actually *could* come across in
your waking experience, but that it would also be *unusual* for
you to do so . . . Now, I'm going to leave you alone to concentrate . . . begin to see the object . . . (20 seconds) . . . see it
clearly, in color . . . keep noticing new things about it . . . see
every detail . . . *hold* it, there, in your mind, in a natural, relaxed
manner . . . (20 seconds) . . . now, see it in your hands, or put

yourself there with it in some way . . . (15 seconds) . . . now, simply *let go* of it . . . watch it fade away . . . disappear it . . . see only the black . . . and when you are ready, begin slowly to let the light of this room seep into your eyelids . . ."

Instruct students to pair up and, for 1 minute, each tells another about their dream. (2 minutes)

Now, hold a brief total-group brainstorm of I — statements (I say, I felt, I think, I couldn't, I wanted to, I liked, I wonder, etc.)

Lastly, instruct the class thusly . . .

"I want each of you, now, to *expect to see your object or other event,* to actually be ready to meet it or come across it. This is what I *don't* mean by "expect."

Don't look everywhere for it, in a straining-to-see kind of way. (This simply builds disappointment, and works *against* seeing it.)

Don't set a time limit, or say to yourself, "Where is it? Why haven't I seen it yet?"

Don't keep looking in places of situations you're already thinking you *might* see it. (This also limits; be ready to be surprised.)

Don't ask your partner "have you gotten yours yet?" (Don't bug each other . . . let go and let it happen.)

This is what I *do* mean by "expect" . . .

Whenever you think of it again, hold the object in your mind, for a few seconds, as we did here today. Relax with it. Then, *let go of it again.*

(*Teacher:* Again, conduct this entire experiment in a warm-hearted, "no-big-deal" manner. Call it an experiment — which it is, an experiment in how experience follows beliefs, instead of vice-versa. Put no pressure on people, on results, or no yourself. When someone does object, be ready to witness putdowns and arguments from doubters who, through their need to discount another's experience, show that their own belief systems are threatened by evidence that each of us is quite that much responsible for his/her experience! "Referree" these tiffs, if they occur, simply by reflecting the feelings you hear, in a way that communicates understanding without agree/disagree commitment on your part:

Jerry: "That's bunk!"

You: "Sounds asif you just don't buy it, Jerry." . . . or . . .

Sylvia: "I think Ann cheated. She just lied about 'coming across' that particular stuffed toy at the carnival booth."

You: "You simply don't believe Ann. You think she's out to fool all of us."

Notice that the key here is to focus on the *belief systems of the person resisting.* These kinds of comments on your part not only communicate neutral empathy, they cause all present to realize something, all over again: *Each of us, whether we like it or not, is always buying into something or other, and causing our experience to fit that belief.* This is the major understanding of this entire unit and the essence of personal responsibility: **I create my own reality.** The connections to the issue of personal health and well-being will "make themselves" as you continue with the Activities. The classroom, long after the unit of study is completed, can continue to be a laboratory for the examination of personal beliefs — with no necessity for agreement.

☆

Feeling my own Elegance

Following a brief study of how body cells, at any moment, are constantly replacing themselves, conduct this as a class activity: "Sit quietly. Close your eyes. Relax. Simply *let go* of any stressful, or angry, or guilty, or fearful thoughts or feelings . . . Turn your attention to *feeling* how each part of your body *knows just exactly how to be itself,* with no effort, strain or conflict at all . . . Your bones somehow know how to be bones, your heart knows, all by itself, just how to beat, and to force the lifegiving red blood throughout your body . . . the lungs, on their own, breathe and breathe, easily, giving you life each moment . . . your brain could not stop thinking even if it wanted to . . . all your body parts work, just now and just now and just now . . . in complete harmony . . . let yourself enjoy, just now for a few relaxed moments, how your organism knows how to be and replace itself in health and harmony . . . ."

(Encourage students to practice this meditative activity early each day or at stressful times. Repeat the activity occasionally in class.)

For Further Study

Here is a list of topics related to the unit theme that represent possibilities for further student research. Ditto the list, have students choose partners, and take "sign-ups" by pairs, as to first, second and third — choice topics for 2- or 3-week study, resulting in written or oral presentations.

What's Going on?

Topics:

__ Biofeedback

__ The function of relaxation in human effectiveness

__ Strength reserves through jogging

__ Strength reserves through meditating

__ Groups that have used the Holistic-Health principle Sufis, Fakirs, Scientism, etc.)

__ T'AI CHI: Chinese Way to health through movement meditation

__ Dreaming your way to health: the ways of the Trobiand islanders.

__ The current holistic-health movement in medicine

__ Acupuncture/acupressure

__ Hypnosis in healing

__ Self-hypnosis in healing

Being Well

__ Vitamin C — *does* it prevent/treat the common cold?

__ Vitamins as preventive health

__ Diet as preventive health

__ Vegetarianism

__ The "jock cult" as national health phenomenon

__ Stress and its effects

__ Noise pollution and its effects

__ Stress-reduction programs in industry

__ How to choose an environment (physical, social, work, etc.) that keeps you healthy

__ ESP and health

__ Yoga and health

__ Bates method of better vision

__ Homeopathy

__ Light and color healing

__ Alleopathic disease: diseases caused by medical treatment

__ The Alexander Technique

__ Chiropratic Medicine

__ Kinesilogy and healing

__ Touch to Heal

A Partial List of Study Resources * *

The Nature of Personal Reality, Roberts
The Long-Run Solution, Henderson
The Well Body Book, Bennett
Be Well, Samuels, Bennett
The Relaxation Response, Benson
Better Eyesight Without Glasses, Bates
The Psychology of Consciousness, Ornstein
How Your Mind Can Keep You Well
The Joy of Running
Powers of Mind, Smith
The Natural Mind, Wiel
The Crack in the Cosmic Egg, Pearce

* These books have significantly influenced the authors in getting this unit together.

* * see bibliography

Beyond Self

Introduction

Students gather before you daily to learn, study and interact. Your dream is that they "get it" before they leave your classroom for good. "Getting it" might mean understanding the concepts of your discipline or discovering more of who they are or isolating problems they want to work on or remembering the facts about Argentina. Each teacher sets goals for the students who assemble each day.

The mission which you took as a teacher is to reach students in their wholeness. You not only have a body but a brain; not only feelings but spirituality; not only a mind but a will. The parts of the student represent a greater whole and the whole student becomes our task as teachers.

We have been discovering the greater connection that exists for us between mind and feelings, between body and spirit. When the body experiences something, so does the mind. Humans are so inter-connected that learning no longer can be considered purely a brain function.

The title of this unit "Beyond Self," was chosen to indicate that there are places to go in education which outreach the self we've generally dealt with in classrooms. The unit is designed to introduce you to some of the current activities in "Transpersonal Education." Areas which are included are relaxation techniques, dreams, healing, meditation, energy and centering. While most of what is suggested here may be new to many of you, it has been done for centuries by great masters in both East and West. There are many ways to tap into the universal knowledge that all of us have. Our minds are far larger than we have suspected. The "New Age" is here. The activities in this section are a few steps into this age.

Important resources for further study are included in the bibliography.

Purposes:

- to begin to understand that the "transpersonal" self is as useful and powerful as any other self in us

- to have students discover how they can use their transpersonal self to learn and experience themselves more fully

- to accept the world of spirituality as an important aspect of humanity

- to become more relaxed and satisfied with living

- to experience a classroom where people love and care for themselves and others

Definition

Introduce the notion of a variety of "selves" within each of us, as:

        Physical self
        Emotional self
        Intellectual self
        Personal Integrative Self (Social)
        Intuitive Self
        Psychical self
        Mystical self
        Transpersonal self
        Volitional Self
        Spiritual Self

Have students define the function of each of these "selves" in a brainstorm.

Have them give examples of where and how they use their different selves during the course of a day.

Discussion Starters

- Find an article in the newspaper or a book which tells of someone using psychic powers (ESP — Futuring) to discover something or someone, or predict an event. Have your students discuss this power. Where does it come from? How come some have more than others? Have you met anyone who is in touch with ESP kind of things?

- Speak to a person who has experienced a "healing." This may be someone of a local religious group or someone who practices healing in other ways. Discuss the origins of the healing power. Try to differentiate whether the healing source is from within or without us. What are the conditions of healing for different people?

- Invite to your class a person who does Transcendental Meditation. Ask them to show you how to meditate. Find out what they receive from this practice. In what ways does it help them day-to-day?

- Discuss the differences between spirituality and being religious.

- Try this:

    Close your eyes and watch your body in your mind, as if you were scanning yourself with a TV camera. Move attention very slowly across your body. Notice where your camera stops and starts; where does it hesitate?

    Discuss — Watching yourself can give you information that can be helpful.

Beyond Self

Circletime

- Dreams I have where I'm doing something I can't normally do

- A problem I solved in my dreams

- Places where I feel most relaxed

- A time I decided to change a feeling and I did

- How my energy changes around different people

- When I walk alone I think of _____

- There are times when I know what is going to happen

- I had a problem that solved itself without help from anyone

- The way I pay attention to myself

- How I practice watching others

- How I know when I'm relaxed

- A time I wish I was relaxed and wasn't

- A favorite daydream I have

Journals

- For the next week record in depth any night dreams that you have. Do you notice any patterns? Are there any similarities in them? Become the characters in your dreams. How are you like them? How are they like you?

- Record any day dreams you have for the next week. Do the same questions as above. In what way are day dreams and night dreams the same/different? What is the significance of each?

- In your journal — describe the things that you'd like to know about in the future — your personal future. Consider that that future moment is out there waiting to happen and you (in your sub/unconcious) already "know" what will happen. What difference does that make to you?

- Think about the possibility of communicating with someone on a dimension other than the physical plane. There is no time, no words, only thoughts, feelings, images sensing. How would you respond to that?

Forced Choice

Would you rather:

- read about something or see something

- relax by running or relax by meditating

What do you get more out of:

- day dreaming or night dreaming

Would you rather:

- read a book or sleep

- think a thought or feel a feeling

- wish a wish or dream a dream

- act as if or feel depressed

Activities

Hand Energy

Pair off your students. Have them sit facing each other with the palms of their hands facing each other but not touching. Ask them to get close but not touch and notice what happens. (You will probably get remarks like, "it's getting warm," or "I feel heat between our hands.")

Ask them:

> Why do you suppose it gets warm?
>
> What is the cause of the heat?
>
> What does this indicate is going on between you and your partner?
>
> Describe how your energy field is like your circulation system.

☆

Meditation

Have each student decide on a sound or word or phrase that they will repeat over and over to themselves. After you have gone through a relaxation activity, have them spend several minutes doing "no thinking" only repeating their word(s) or sound.

After your students have "meditated" ask them:

> What are the things you did to keep yourself on your sound?

On a "relaxed" continuum are you more or less relaxed than when we started?

What did you find hard — what did you find easy?

Share your feelings as you were doing this.

☆

Relaxation and Centering

(Note: Most of the activities in this section will be prefaced by some form of relaxation technique. A person's state of mind is a major variable on how well she performs. If she is tense and controlled the experience will reflect that. If the person is relaxed she will probably have more insight and enlightenment. Relaxation can be self-induced. The research that is being done in bio-feedback and bio-energetics indicates that we are our own controllers. Drugs induce a false control — all of us can learn how to control not only our grosser movements but also our more subtle rhythm, heart-beat, brainwaves and electrical fields.)

The following are some ways to direct people to relax themselves:

• *Float:* Close your eyes and see yourself floating on your back in a warm pool of water. You are buoyant and won't sink. Accept and experience the sensations of the gently moving water and sun.

• *Count Breaths:* Close your eyes and start counting your breaths. Start to make the breaths come slower and deeper so that you are counting less often.

- *Tighten and Relax:* Close your eyes and starting with your toes — tighten your muscles and relax them — move upward using this method on each group of muscles. (Teacher: they can do this on their own or with your direction. If they go slowly they achieve a more relaxed state.)

- *Lower Breathing:* Close your eyes. See a line drawn from your navel to your mouth. Place the numbers 1-10 on the line (10 at your mouth). Begin to focus on your breathing, how "deep" it is, how far down the line it goes. After several breaths say to yourself — "take it down one number and 'lower,' or deepen your breathing one number on the scale." After several breaths say it again. (Students can learn to do this on their own.)

- *Centering:* Close your eyes and get your number on your breathing line. Drop your number one at a time until you feel relaxed. From that number on your line go slowly into your body until you find a place that feels like the center between your back and front. Experience that center as your energy source. All the things that go on in your body are flowing from that point. Enlarge the center slightly and relax in the feeling you get. Get a word or sound to say over and over to yourself. Feel yourself relax and experience your center with the word or sound.

Some of the benefits from relaxation are physical. Relaxation gives a person a chance to revitalize quickly. Students can use it to release tension before tests or athletic competition, or before giving a speech. Sometimes when you are being confronted you can become less defensive if you "relax on the spot." It's practice in paying attention to yourself and exercising control.

☆

Going Away

Bodies have many parts to them. When you ride in an elevator that starts quickly you may sense your body leaving and coming back quickly. When you are about to sleep you may "jerk" just before you fall off and wake yourself. This is another example of what seems like your body leaving and then coming back quickly — thus the jerk.

That part of your body is called by some the etheral body.

Another part of your body is the "astral" part. It is able to send thoughts through the air waves to other places and in one sense to "be there." (In an astral sense, not a physical sense.) When people think strongly about someone they usually "project" themselves to that person.

Have your students close their eyes going through some relaxation activities and begin to think of someone else. Have them stay with that one person — not wandering around but focusing on one individual for several minutes.

After a few minutes have them —

- Share some of the feelings they had as they were doing this

- Were there any surprises they got?

- Have them check later if the other person actually "got" anything from them

(As they learn to send their energy to others, others will begin to feel that energy.)

☆

Planned Projection

This is an activity which can be done to practice using your astral body to "go" places. In your home pick out a place you want to go to that's some distance from where you sleep. Walk that distance at least six times to notice everything that is there as you go from your bed to your destination. The next time you walk it, pick out six specific points. Identity places — places to remember — on your walk. Remember those places clearly. Picture them in your mind. The next evening as you are going to sleep see yourself walking from your bed to your destination by "going" to those six points. Go over them again and again and suggest to yourself that while you sleep you will "go" there. (This is an activity that needs practice.)

After some of your students have done this for some time have them share some of their experiences. Help them to learn to trust their whole bodies. They may go somewhere they hadn't expected. Reflect their experience to them and hear what meaning they receive from their "trips." They are starting to be in touch with the connections they already have between their physical and non-physical selves.

☆

Messages

Pick a day when you will decide that everything that happens to you is a message to you from someplace. Each message you get is a gift to you and says something noble about you. Because of the messages you receive you can be a stronger, better person that day.

Watch yourself smile most of the day.

Guided Fantasy

- You are standing at the end of a long tunnel. You start to walk through the tunnel. Record the things you hear and see and smell and touch.

- You have become the rain. Experience in detail what you do as the rain.

- You are scuba diving in the ocean. This is your chance to experience the depths of ocean life. Take your trip.

- You are digging a hole in the earth. Experience yourself going deeper and deeper into the earth. Look up and see the sky through this hole in the earth.

- You can walk into fire and not get injured. Ahead of you you see a large fire burning. Walk into it and see the world through the fire.

- Close your eyes and get comfortable. See the sun as a bright light shining on you. Watch how you change because of the bright light.

- Close your eyes. In your mind's eye see three people you know very well. They could be parents, siblings, friends. Pick three. Look at each person, one at a time, very closely. Study their faces, the way they stand, the kinds of clothes they wear, the general impression they give you.

  Now gradually replace their face with your face and feel what it is like to be in their bodies. Go slowly so that you can feel what "being them" is like; watch yourself being them.

Process:

In which body were you most comfortable?

What were some of the things which distracted you as you were going from body to body?

How would you change yourself to feel different in your new bodies?

How are you like all those bodies?

What kind of different thoughts did you have as different people?

Brainstorm

- Ways to solve a problem by depending on your feelings

- The uses of your intuition

- How to get people to become more aware of themselves

- The uses of quiet time

- How to get people to be honest with themselves

- Ways to be more healing towards each other

- How to create an energy pool for people who are low on energy

- How the sun could be used to create peace in the world

Role Plays

There are six roles to this play:

> The Intellect
> The Intuition
> The Senses
> The Emotions
> The Will
> The Spirit

Give each person some time to figure out how they will act in one of the following "scripts."

- You have the choice to be involved in two different activities, one takes risk, the other none at all.

- There is an important person coming to spend some time in your home.

- You've been asked on a date by someone you admire, or dislike.

- Someone said something you were just about to say.

- You forgot an important meeting.

- Someone didn't keep their word.

Process:

Process each activity so that your students get a clearer idea of those different parts of them that are always responding to any situation.

Inventories

- Make a list of the kinds of dreams you have.

    Code them:

  > S —strength dreams
  >
  > R —running dreams.
  >
  > A —afraid dreams.
  >
  > F —falling dreams.
  >
  > P —proud dreams.
  >
  > X —sexual dreams.
  >
  > —others

- Make a list of things that you like to do.

    Coding:

  > M — takes more mind than will to do this.
  >
  > F — takes more feelings than mind to do this.
  >
  > W — takes more will than feelings to do this.
  >
  > — others

• Think of things that you would like to accomplish in the next year.

   Code them by using the following:

   P —physical activity

   L —has to do with learning something

   R —a recreational activity

   T —will take thought and planning

   W — you'll have to use a great amount of will power to accomplish this

   S —this will be spiritually uplifting for you

• List how you give yourself strokes, compliments, praise.

   Coding:

   T —I treat myself to something new

   W —I use words

   O —I get others to pat me on the back

   D —I daydream of how good I am

Body

Introduction

How is it that consciousness resides in our bodies? Thousands of times each day, they change with the constant formation of cells and tissues and yet each "I" appears constant to itself. With the trick of filing experiences we call "memory," and with the experience of time as linear, we seem to see our bodies "grow" and "mature." Living in our bodies as we do, it is never clear whether the "I in here" is separate or the same as the "Not-I out there," or whether I am *in* my body or *am* my body. The notion has had long acceptance, with both natural and behavioral scientists, that each of us *forms* and *maintains* his or her body. Each body can be seen to be the net result, at any one moment, of how the person *notions* himself or of herself. (This theory is not only unchallenged, but corroborated by the discontents most of us feel and express about the way we look — simply more acting-out of self-denial.) Thus, "She's not comfortable with her body" is code that translates, "She's forming and maintaining a body to be uncomfortable in." Body-image is not only something each of us *originates,* it can be changed — and the body changed as a result! The body unit activities can begin to open children's awareness of their *choices* concerning their own organism.

71

Body

Purposes

- To dispel awe of one's own body, promote ownership, proprietership, ease and familiarity with it

- To acquaint students with their own responsibility to themselves, by means of their bodies

- To develop trust in one's own intuitive knowing and behaving

- To allow each student to *redo* his definition of his body, by dispelling definitions that are based on judgement

- To allow each student to *re-experience* the body, learn to learn from it, and make decisions to alter it if these are desirable

Definition

- *Brainstorm:* "The body is . . ." for 10 minutes with the class, and write all endings on newsprint. Have them help you group, code, or find patterns in the list. (Some codes: J for judgement (+/−), D for dwelling, I for identity, etc.)

- *Anonymous:* Have each student use "disguised writing" to print three endings to the phrase "My body is . . ." and collect the papers. Share by posting, reading aloud or doing "What things seem to come up again and again that tell about our *feelings* about our bodies? Do we seem to basically like and accept them?"

- *Collage Bulletin Board:* or mural entitled "What is (the) body?" or "How is it where *you* live?" Ask students to contribute items that would appear to them to be useful in explaining to a non-encorporated spacebeing *what it is like to be in a body.*

72

Body

- Select experiences from the following list of books: *

  Centering Book
  The New Games Book
  Gimme Something to Feel

  Stop a Moment
  Second Centering Book

  * see bibliography

- *Watching Roleplays*

  Have class pretend classroom is a spaceship from planet
  Splook that has just landed on this planet, called earth.
  Students are Splookans who are investigating inhabitants
  of Earth. While certain detoxification and immigration
  procedures are being carried out, class will get its first
  look at earthlings, by watching "this box they all watch"
  (turning on TV). Tell class we'll watch without sound,
  "since their sounds are unknown to us anyway," and that
  they are to pretend they know nothing about earthling
  activities or culture, except that they are watching earthlings' bodies do what it is earthlings do. "Ask
  yourselves:

  - What do they seem to be doing?

  - What do they want?

  - What is important to them?

  - How do their bodies express their existence?"

  Then, with no sound on, turn through several one- or two-
  minute segments for variety, including, if possible,
  commercials, soap operas, game shows, and old movies.

Body

Discussion Starters

• "In the next 60 seconds each of you is to make as long a list as you can, of *things you like to do.* Go!" After the brainstorm, have lists coded B for body, and have kids rewrite the extrapolated list in rank-order — from most important to least. "What comes up for you, about your relationship with your body? Let's use, 'I learned that I . . .' in sharing aloud."

• *Are* you your body OR are you *in* your body? After giving a minute to ponder the question, have youngsters line-up on one or two opposite "forced-choice" sides of the room according to their answers to it. Give a minute for "teams" to talk about why they chose as they did. *Directions:* "Now, each get together with someone from the *other* team for a 4-minute debate on this question. Each of you in your dyad, the "body" and the "in-your-body," has two minutes. "Bodies" first. Ready? Go!"

• Other issues:

＿ Do you control your body OR does "it" control you?

＿ How are you your body, and how are you not your body?

＿ Where do you "go" when you die? Is a dead body still a person?

＿ Where did you come from? Why?

＿ In what sense are you "always alone" in your body?

＿ When you eat your food becomes part of your body. How is that part the same/different that what was your body?

＿ How does your body have and live its own history?

Body

Circletime

- My feelings about my body

- Three things I like about my body

- Something about my body I wish I could change

- How I think my body "suits me"

- Something about my body I could forgive if I would

- The perfect body

- A recent change I notice in my body

- How others' bods look to me

- How I use TV bodies to judge my own

- The best I remember feeling

- A time I know I *am* my body (know I'm not)

- How I learn and use "control" of my body

- How my body "does" me

- How I experience things

- What I do to know my body

- Thoughts about my body I think often

Body

Journal Entries

• *Zero-to-ten scales*

Give yourself a number, from zero (nothing) to ten (everything, all, entirely) on . . .

_ I accept myself

_ I accept my body

_ How I rate my body on its:

    ___ height

    ___ weight

    ___ build

    ___ facial characteristics

    ___ beauty

    ___ coloring (skin, hair, eyes, etc.)

    ___ complexion

    ___ grace

    ___ strength

    ___ health

    ___ physical abilities

    ___ ease

    ___ general attractiveness

    ___ general grade it gets

Body

- *Influences*

    I get my ideas and attitudes about my body mostly from:

    ____ myseif

    ____ my parents

    ____ my friends

    ____ society

    ____ TV, media

    ____ other (what?_____)

- *Breathing Scale*

    On a scale of zero (so shallow you're panting like a dog) to 10 (deepness of deep, relaxed sleep) — where is your breathing right now? — What happens if your concentrate, just now, on "lowering" it one notch (next highest number)?

- *Here-and-now-wheel*

    Draw a wheel and divide it in four. "Scan" your body with your awareness, and find your feelings you're experiencing, right here, now. Put them down. Now, star one and write a short statement about it.

Example:

* I know I'm partly "tuned out" because I was up late last night, but that's also okay with me.

Body

Teacher: Create scales (0-10, pie graphs, or zero-center continuums) with which students can rate themselves each day,
continually, in their journals. Examples: "Open your journals
and give yourself a number, zero-to-ten, on where your energy
level is right now, (zero means you're passed out on the floor,
and ten means you're climbing the walls)." This could be all to
get students to practice one more dimension of the body -
awareness-scanning skill . . . or, you could have kids note
which behaviors of theirs are outgrowths of that energy level:
ask everyone to change to another seat in the room, and then
assess energy level again; ask "How do our bodies reflect our
mental state?"; etc.

Roleplays

•   *Role reversal:*

    Students choose partners to "become each other" and
    simulate a two-minute conversation. Emphasize "body
    language" — sitting, moving, gesturing and moving face
    — as mimicking task proceeds. After two minutes, part-
    ners stop and process. (How did I see me in you? How did
    I see you in me? What new perceptions do I have of
    myself?)

•   Play the game *Roll-a-Role* (available from Mandala Press).

•   *Slow Motion Mirroring:*

    Partners stand or sit, facing each other. One is the
    "leader." the other the "mirror." Leader moves slowly.
    After a minute, without a break, ask them to reverse roles.
    Then to "pass" leader role back and forth, intuitively,
    without talking, then to "lose" roles and still continue.
    Discuss the activity as a form of dance. What *is* dance?
    How is *conflict* a sort of dance?

Body

Inventories

- "Track" one's attention for 2 minutes, writing down each thing one notices. Code list, with OB (outside-body) and IB (inside-body).

- 10 "improvements" I'd make on my body

- 3 things I could *consciously do* to make *each* of the ten items above so

- 5 changes I note when I am afraid (5 ways I tense my body when I scare myself)

- Things my body does to tell me it is sick (tired, under pressure, etc.)

- "Messages" I get from 5 bodies around me now — followed by at least two ways to check each out

- People I know or know about (i.e. see on TV, etc.) whose bodies "play" uptight (loose, wary, angry, lovely, etc.)

- Things my body is feeling while I do this

Forced Choice

Would you rather be . . .

- male OR female?
- short OR tall?
- old OR young?
- fat OR skinny?
- quick OR slow-moving?
                . . .why?

Body

Which is more vital to you?

- seeing OR hearing?
- arms OR legs?
- relaxing OR tensing?
- what else?

Which is worse?

- having to sit still a long time OR
  having to exert yourself for a long time?
- emotional pain OR physical pain?
- being angry OR being afraid?
- being sore or being tired?

Do you experience your body as more of a . . .

- snake OR cabbage?
- moon OR sun?
- tree OR fish?
- cube OR sphere?
- mountain OR sea?
- Tuesday OR Sunday?
- green OR orange?
- solid OR liquid?
- water OR ice?
- sunshine OR moonshine?
- coke OR 7-up?
- what else?

Right now, does your body feel . . .

- up OR down?
- in OR out?
- far OR near?
- standing OR running?
- rough OR smooth?
- silver OR gold?
  - . . . let your *body* give the answers!

Body

Rank Order

• The five senses in value to you

• The parts of the body

• Body characteristics (use list of 0-10 scales, under *journals*)

• Your 5 "favorite bods" anywhere

• Rate the following in body . . .

____ Fonzie	____ Farah Fawcett Majors
____ Barbara Walters	____ Kotter
____ Kojak	____ Edith Bunker
____ John-Boy	____ Muhammed Ali
____ Bionic Woman	____ Other (Who?)

• Rank-order these things for you to do with your body, from "What I do most of" to "What I do least of" . . .

____ examining	____ putting-down
____ enjoying	____ using (like a tool)
____ forgetting about	____ thinking about
____ worrying about	____ admiring
____ showing off	____ caring for
____ experiencing	____ loving
____ fearing	____ other? _____

Body

- From "worst" to "least worst" . . . feeling . . .

___ frustrated	___ sick
___ helpless	___ afraid
___ hurt	___ annoyed
___ angry	___ worried
___ tense	___ ready to fight
___ ready to run	___ ready to explode

(Code each feeling for the "Where?" _____ the *part* of the body in which each feeling is experienced).

Spectrums

- Give yourself a number . . .

$$-5 \quad -4 \quad -3 \quad -2 \quad -1 \quad 0 \quad +1 \quad +2 \quad +3 \quad +4 \quad +5$$

HATES	LOVES
1. his/her body	his/her body
2. totally laid-back	totally up-tight
3. ugly body	beautiful body
4. super-weak body	super-strong body

. . . etc.

Body

- Where Are You on an energy scale of 0 to 10, when you are:

____ in class   ____ at home

____ at a dance   ____ when "up in front," performing

____ right now   ____ before a date

____ in a fight   ____ watching TV

____ sleeping   ____ with family

____ on the phone   ____ others . . .

- Talk with a Partner for one minute about your choice of a number from this chart . . .

　　　　1 — strongly agree
　　　　2 — agree
　　　　3 — agree and disagree
　　　　4 — disagree
　　　　5 — strongly disagree

. . . after I read each of these statements; tell your partner your number and *why* you feel as you do . . .

____ You are totally alone, inside your skin (discuss in 2's using scale)

____ All sickness is either consciously or unconsciously chosen

____ You can't really get hurt

____ Being right doesn't work

____ All "healing" is done by the sick person

____ You always see what you expect to see

Brainstorms

- ways to relax

- ways to learn from yourself

- ways to heal yourself

- favorite ways to exercise

- all the ways to prove there is no such thing as "time"

- peak experiences

- names for the body

- names for the self

- places you experience energy in a special way

- improvements you could make on the body

- ways to listen to your body

Body

Whips

- My body _____-s for me.

- I clutch up when _____ .

- I sometimes experience tension in _____ (part of body).

- Sometimes by body knows better than I do, that _____ .

- A favorite part of my body is my _____ .

- I like the way my body _____ .

- I'm not so crazy about my _____ (part of body).

- Wish I had a body like _____.

- I use my body most when I _____ .

Guided Fantasy

- *Out-of-body-Trip*

  "Relax and uncross your body . . . (eight seconds' pause
  for each set of three dots) . . . let your eyes close, and
  forget about people and events around you for a moment .
  . . find a silent place inside of you, and go there . . . be
  alone, with yourself . . ., . . ., . . ., . . .

  Now imagine that you are able, somehow, easily, and
  without effort, to temporarily to place your body on "hold"
  for a while, and just bring your awareness somewhat
  outside and apart from your breathing, relaxing body, so
  that you can *see* it, sitting there . . . now, move your
  awareness to the other side of your body, and look at it
  from that angle . . . and now, from directly above your
  body, at the ceiling level . . . and now, place your
  awareness back into your body . . . and now place it just
  behind your eyelids, and watch what happens as they
  open . . ."

- *Body Trip*

  (Use the introduction from the above fantasy, or
  something like it, to induce relaxation and concentration
  first.)" . . . Now, I want you to imagine that you can put
  your big, breathing, relaxing body on automatic, and that
  you can somehow, separately, by concentrating and
  restricting your awareness, become very, very, small . . .
  and find yourself *inside* your body somewhere . . . now, I'm
  going to give you some time to take a very enjoyable trip
  inside your body . . . you can sit any place you like . . .
  (wait 1½ minutes) . . .

  . . . Now, begin to bring your awareness up, and up, to just
  behind your eyes, so that it is just behind your eyelids,
  looking at them as if they are two blinds, or curtains,
  pulled down . . . and now, feel yourself grow and spread
  throughout your breathing body . . . and watch, as the
  curtains of your eyelids begin to raise . . ."

Body

- *Tension Relaxing Training*

  Following a relaxation-concentration opening, guide students to explore their bodies for any evidence of:

  > fear
  > hurt
  > tension
  > sickness or
  > negative feeling

  After the internal event is located, guide them to focus attention on it by determining silently, each of the following:

  What shape is it?
  What color is it?
  How big, in inches, is it?
  What is it doing?
  What is its surface like?
  How is it changing?
  . . . Watch it . . .

  (If students are "successful" with these techniques, do not be surprised if some wonderingly report loss of headaches, angers, tensions, cramps, or even toothaches. These phenomena can lead to a useful discussion around the question "How are we *always* creating our experience?")

- *Lower Breathing*

  Imagine a zero to ten scale for your breathing and determine the "lowest" point at which you are breathing. Notice, after concentrating for a few moments on this task, how the world looks "different" to you afterwards, if it does. Share this technique with the class, and practice it with them. See if you, or any of them, can remember it when . . .

87

"it's boring"
You are angry or upset
you are about to do a demanding task
you need a break from "drudge"
you are sad
you are scared

Tips: whether eyes are shut or not becomes less of an
issue with practice. Do not try to "mix" your awareness of
the breathing scale with what is going on: the secret is to
"take yourself away" momentarily, by concentrating, and
*give your attention fully to the scale and the task of
lowering the breathing level.*

- *Body Scan*

Next time you think of it, do a "body scan." Run your
awareness briefly and smoothly, throughout your entire
body. Imagine, situated just to the side of your awareness,
a "radar screen" (this can be done with eyes open or
closed), and watch it for any "blip" on the screen, as the
radar scans each area of the body, which may signal . . .

> tension
> hurt
> tingles
> uncomfortableness
> soreness
> need for . . . what? . . .

or other events.

The aware teacher, who has sheared and practices "body
scanning" with students, can plug in the skill at various
times of the teaching day — or ask students to do the
same (*Examples:* SELF: "Okay, my stomach's tight, and it
feels like it's *been* that way a while, and so this started
with me *before* John spilled the eraser shavings . . ." or
". . . OTHER: Phyllis, before we go on arguing, I'd like you
to do a body-scan for me, and share something that you
get."

Activities

Source: Many of the activities in the unit on Being Crazy and Pace (*Strategies in Humanistic Education, Volume 2*) are appropriate for this unit, also.

Silhouettes

Have students work in pairs one lying on the back of a large sheet of paper as other traces around the body. Silhouettes are then cut out and covered with a collage of pictures showing things each body likes. In the head are pictured thoughts and fantasies, in the stomach favorite foods and emotions; arms and legs show activities, etc. Collages may be cardboard-backed, shellacked and stood around the room for display.

Source: Use activities from the movement section, volume 2 of the *Strategies* series.

Watching the Play

Have students practice watching the world, for periods of several minutes, as if everything happening in it were *stages*. Have them pretend that every movement of every person around them is practiced and rehearsed and presented . . . just now, just that way . . . "on cue." This is most easily done as a "peoplewatching" exercise in a fairly crowded public place. Eventually, assign each student to do any individual "watching the play" assignment, spending at least 15 minutes perceiving body language this way, in a mall or store or other well-peopled place.

Body

_____

Note: Once people begin to practice this "trick" of watching the world of others as a drama, they very quickly develop it as a skill of recognition. The ability to watch the movie, while being *in* the movie, is one that enables the perceiver to recognize his own and others' "acts." The more times you structure momentary practice of "watching the play," the more you allow the development of each child's seer.

☆

Watch a Bod

Names in a hat. Each student becomes a secret observer of the person whose name s/he picks, for the remainder of the day or period. Observation is primarily of behavior of the body: "make yourself a TV camera, with the mike turned off." At the end of the time, observers "feed back" what they saw as body language patterns. One or more of the following tasks may be given to the observers at one time:

> How much space does the person observed (O) seem to require or maintain, between O's body, and other bodies or objects?
>
> How much space does O's body occupy in movement (i.e. are gestures broad, restricted, etc.?)
>
> Where does O spend most time in this environment?
>
> Practice seeing O as part of a 'group dance' with the others. What part does O play?
>
> Pretend that O is in a play just now, acting on cue in everything O does. What is O's part?
>
> Pretend that O is an animal that can change itself into other animals at will. What three animals can you find O being?

Body

You may wish to have students make slight notes, or sketches, for information to share with their O's after the observation period. Emphasize at the outset that there will be much more payoff if people will 1) be objective and descriptive (rather than speculative or judgemental in giving feedback) and 2) attempt, as much as possible, to get *totally into watching and totally out of being watched.* In the processing of this activity together, encourage discussion of these, too, as useful observing skills.

Observer Walk

Students lineup in two facing lines, and each takes a turn walking the length of the aisle formed, while lines watch the walker. Share feelings of what it was like to walk the aisle (these are usually uncomfortable, self-conscious). Now, do the walk exercise over again, with one change: each walker is now to put all of his/her attention on others in a very focused way (observe all the chins, or feet, or clothing, or compare the heights of people, look at the shapes of the spaces between them, etc.) Compare feelings of walkers this time with the first. Note that we *always* have the choice, when with others, to watch or be watched.

Practice changing your body

Most of us, in the extremely important (to us) area of personal appearance, are cooperating in a mass self-delusion. As a culture, we have created and perpetuated the notion that things *outside* the body determine the body's appearance. We've contrived models and stereotypes for beauty and ugliness, and a host of cosmetics, all in order to feel powerless, done-to, essentially out of control of how our bodies appear.

Have children conduct an experiment in changing their physical selves:

Body

1. Begin with a class brainstorm on "ways of changing how our bodies look." Code for "changes from *inside*" — attitude, exercise, diet, etc. and "changing from *outside* — clothing, cosmetics. Focus attention on the latter.

2. Suggest the following assumptions for discussion:

    A. Appearance is always a result of options (i.e. you are always choosing how to look).

    B. Our bodies are not something done to us, but organisms that we fully support, maintain, and choose to be in.

    C. Griping about certain things about your body — even regretting them or discounting them in any way — is simply trying to escape what you yourself choose and support.

    D. You can always choose an alternative appearance, and bring it about.

3. Assign kids to keep journals on a project entitled, *Changing the Way I Look.* Throughout the project, kids are practicing choosing alternative appearances — not in style and makeup, but in actual structure of the body. The goal of all this is for each of us to realize, by experiencing how very much in control of this we are.

    Students work in pairs of 3's to contract changes such as body weight, muscular structure, hair, posture, loss of tension, etc. (*Example*: Beginning to run can actually bring about changes in one's body build in a relatively short time.) Groups support, report to and encourage each other.

Body

Methods: Use the brainstorm list to suggest ways to bring these changes about. Supplement with another brainstorm entitled "All the ways we can think of to change your appearance by changing your *mind* . . ." (Items from *each* list should be "requireds" in the contractual obligations kids take upon themselves during this study.)

Set a time frame — such as six weeks — during which each project proceeds. Use written contracts and frequent support-group meetings to encourage attention on the issue.

In the end, assess attitudinal changes that might indicate positive movement on a scale called *How much in charge I feel/how I look.*

Competition/Cooperation

Introduction

In our present societal structure there are many represen-
tations of cooperation. Insurance companies, gas companies,
banks, labor unions, the steel and auto industries all cooperate
out of survival needs. One company does not decide to cut the
prices so drastically to be out of line with the others. There is a
cooperation in competition. In sports and recreation arenas
players cooperate to compete with other teams. Glory emerges
because the team has worked together to beat the other team.
The perfectly executed double play, fast break, or end run
brings cheers. Our society honors the highly cooperative team
in the competitive arena.

Purpose

- to experience the advantages/disadvantages of
  cooperation/competition.

- to make value choices out of understanding of
  cooperation/competition.

- to be able to articulate an understanding of the concepts
  of cooperation/competition.

- to design learning activities to make the classroom a more
  cooperative place.

- to test the appropriateness of cooperation/competition.

- to understand left-right brain in terms of
  cooperation/competition.

Definition

- Have the class make a list of synonyms for the words cooperation — competition.

- Have a cooperation/competition board in the classroom where there is a constant refining of the definition of cooperation/competition through news articles etc.

- Have students interview some adults to get their definitions of cooperation/competition.

Discussion Topics

React:

- athletic teams have decided to play games for entertainment rather than to see who wins. They no longer keep score.

- the government controls all prices so that consumers and producers are treated fairly.

- Communism/capitalism as they relate to cooperation/competition.

- consumers need to cooperate in order to control the producers.

- how can we cooperate and compete in our classroom

- we have the responsibility to set up a cooperative council in our school. What will we do?

- is there any correlation between competition and physical contact?

- everyone wins in cooperation.

Circletime topics

- 1. I competed and won.
- 2. I competed and lost.
- 3. I competed and it was tie.
- 4. The difference between competing alone or with others
- 5. The feelings I have when I compete and when I cooperate
- 6. I was working with cooperative people . . . . .
- 7. When I'm feeling little and those around me seem big . . . .
- 8. Places where I feel most competitive/cooperative
- 9. A time I got beat and had been highly competitive
- 10. A time I won and had been highly competitive
- 11. A time I lost and had been highly cooperative
- 12. A time I won and had been highly cooperation
- 13. I wanted to win because . . . . .
- 14. I dislike/like competition because _____
- 15. A lesson I learned from cooperating/competing
- 16. I was a winner and no one noticed me.
- 17. I was a loser and everyone noticed me.
- 18. The behavior I think represents competition/cooperation
- 19. I remember a time when others cooperated with me
- 20. How I cooperate with my body

Journal Entries

- I wish I could win at _____ .

- The times when I feel very inadequate as a competitor

- Sentences I say to myself when I lose

- A friend of mine didn't cooperate with me

- Some goals I have to cooperate with others

- Some of the things I don't understand about cooperation/competition

- When I'm relaxed I usually (cooperate or compete) more?

- The things I don't like about cooperation

- The things I don't like about competition

Forced Choice

___ I'd rather win after a hard fight
    OR
___ I'd rather win after an easy fight.

___ I'd rather lose by a lot
    OR
___ I'd rather lose by a little.

I have a greater sense of accomplishment if I:

___ work alone OR
___ with others

___ plan alone OR
___ plan with others

Competition/Cooperation

— learn a skill on my own OR
— get help from a skilled person.

— know the outcome of our efforts OR
— have to depend on others to know the outcome.

Competition implies   Cooperation implies

Competition implies	Cooperation implies
— more struggle OR — more accomplishment.	— more struggle OR — more accomplishment.
— more planning OR — more achievements.	— more planning OR — more achievement
— more security OR — more risks.	— more security OR — more risks.
— more losers OR — more winners.	— more losers OR — more winners.

Rank Order

Rank the following in your order of preference: —
Rank them — competitive to noncompetitive (1 - 5)
Rank them — physical contact to non-physical contact (A - E)

____ football   ____ volleyball

____ soccer   ____ badminton

____ hockey   ____ other (what? _____)

____ basketball

____ baseball

____ ping pong

____ jogging

____ distance running

Competition/Cooperation

Place these in order of amount of cooperation each demands

____ building a house

____ sailing a boat

____ planting a garden

____ raising a pet

____ solving a problem

____ deciding on watching a TV program

Who represents cooperation/competition more?

____ police person

____ teacher

____ parent

____ doctor

____ son/daughter

____ president

Why do people compete?

____ They have to

____ It feels good

____ It brings attention, recognition

____ It helps make friends

____ They're afraid

____ It prevents trouble

____ They get more of what they want

____ Other (what?)

Competition/Cooperation

Why do people cooperate

____ They have to

____ It feels good

____ It brings attention, recognition

____ It helps make friends

____ They're afraid

____ It prevents trouble

____ They get more of what they want

____ other (what?)

Spectrum

• The success of team sports is that one team competes against another.

• The results of most competition is positive.

• When people work together they are stronger.

• Our classroom is a place of cooperation.

• The reason people cooperate is that they are afraid.

• Competition with self is more important than competition with others.

• In a classroom where competition prevails usually more gets done.

• I'm more of a cooperator than competitor.

Whips

- A winner is _____ .

- If I could compete in something, I'd _____ .

- Something I'd like to win is _____ .

- What I enjoy cooperating in is _____ .

- In order to be a winner you have to _____ .

- When a team wins it _____ .

- A loser is _____ .

Role Plays

Set up a scene where someone won't share-processes. Partners sit facing each other. One has something the other wants, and won't share. (Open-ended roleplay for 2 minutes, then reverse roles). Repeat with a version where the "item" is shared. Process in terms of comparative feelings, thoughts and behaviors.

Activities

☆

Family Cooperation:

List at least five things in your family that require cooperation. Which of these do you relate to? How come cooperation is needed? When people don't cooperate what happens?

☆

Left-Right:

Teacher: the left brain is analytical, reasonable, logical, evaluative and critical. The right brain is intuitive, flowing, goalless, creative, imaginative and non-critical. To learn a skill without self-doubt the right brain needs to function. Have your students listen to left-right statements in their minds as they throw tennis balls to each other. If you hear:

> I missed
> Darn!
> If I could only
> I missed again
> > — that's "left"

If you hear:

> I feel it
> I'm loving it
> It's beautiful
> Look at the grace and flow
> It looks like a (bird)
> > — That's "right."

Practice in right brain helps people flow into cooperation and greater satisfaction in skill development.

☆

Right Practice:

Play basketball (volleyball, tennis, ping pong, etc.) without using the ball. After the game, ask the students who won or if anyone missed a shot. Have them close their eyes at their seats and see themselves enjoying doing a skill. Ask them — do they do better than expected? (Teacher: when people fantasize they don't criticize themselves — they excel.)

☆

Skill Development:

Have students choose a skill they'd like to get better at. When they have chosen, have them close their eyes and lead them through the following guided fantasy: "See yourself approaching the time when you are going to do what you want to get better at . . . . . Begin the tasks . . . . . watch yourself complete the task . . . . . begin the task again and this time see yourself doing what you're doing in show motion. As you do it see yourself doing it better than before . . . . . next see yourself excelling in what you are doing. You don't fail, you succeed . . . . . Watch yourself doing it slow . . . . . fast . . . . . slow . . . . . fast . . . . . regular . . . . . very slow . . . . . Walk away and come back to the classroom. Open your eyes."

Teacher: Process by asking:

How do you feel about doing your skill?
Can you do it better than before ? How do you know?
What if you tried (try) your skill and things aren't any better?
Give them time to try their skill — to get some immediate feedback.

☆

Ring Toss:

Get several ring toss games. Place them 10 feet away and have
each student toss 5 rings. Keep score. After each has had a
turn, have them set a goal of how many they will ring out of 15
tosses. Have them do it and compare goal to accomplishment.
Do a fantasy as in "Skill Development" activity and do the task
again. What's the difference and why?

☆

Newspaper and Competition

Watch the newspapers for several weeks and collect all the
examples you can of competition and cooperation. Do you find
more cooperation or competition in:

> government
> sports
> feature acticles
> domestic affairs
> international affairs
> family/society section
> Editorials
> market and economics

Process: What does this indicate to you?
    What can be done to make changes?

☆

Non-Judgmental time:

Set aside a certain time each day where you have your
students think thoughts of cooperation. After several days
check in with your students on whether it makes a difference
to take the time to "think" cooperation.

Fear

Introduction

The usual thing people say when they are afraid is
" _____ really scares me" or "When you do this you scare
me." The focus of the scare seems to be outside of them.
Whereas fearing is an *inner* event. We cause our own fear by
giving something outside ourselves power over us. Thus: "I'm
afraid" means — "I'm afraiding myself" or "I'm scaring
myself."

Fear is a major limiter to humans. Running scared from the
world stops people, freezes people, causes them to get sick
and even die. The truth is that most people are more afraid of
you than you are of others. Most of the things that are "scary"
have their impact because we *let* them impact.

The goal of this section is to identify some of the ways people
scare themselves, seek some alternatives and plan some
strategies to BOO the world instead of being BOOED by it.

Fear

Purposes

- to discover that people who are scaring themselves usually cover up their fear with an act that masks the fear

- to re-experience the fears that we have in order to confront them and see them vanish

- to see that fears are ways to handle the world

- to seek strategies for not resisting fear

- to practice living in the NOW rather than the scary past or future.

Discussion Starters

- Everyone is more afraid of you than you are of them.

- The only time we have is the time that is now. We can't do anything about the future except plan for it or worry about it.

- If everyone was less afraid we'd have more joyful times.

- The major reason for arguments between people is that people are afraid of each other.

- Why are people afraid of people who have the role of:

    Police officers
    Government officials
    Internal Revenue Services personnel
    Psychiatrists/Psychologists
    Doctors

Fear

- What does guilt have to do with fear?

- Discuss times when you were in a new situation. Describe how you scared yourself.

- What does self-consciousness have to do with being afraid?

- If we knew the future we would be afraid.

- Fear has suddenly ceased to exist in everyone — what does the world act like now?

- Why do you suppose people choose fear instead of another emotion at certain times?

Circletime Topics

- How I scare myself with my friends

- A time I scared myself with an adult

- My body tells me about my scaries

- A time I was scared and confronted my scaries

- When I'm afraid I usually _____

- An accident happened where I was afraid

- A dream I have that is scary

- The reason I scare myself is usually _____

- I was new and scared myself

Fear

- When I was new I scared myself by _____

- I'm angry about _____ and that implies I'm scared of _____

Whips

- I'm afraid when _____ .

- Fear is _____ .

- Things that scare me most are _____ .

- The way to not be afraid is _____ .

- If everyone _____ , fear would go away.

- A fear I remember from childhood is _____ .

- What I do to control my fear is _____ .

- If _____ happens I'll scare myself.

Role Plays

• Someone who knows more than you is coming in to correct your work.

• The principal has just called you to the office.

• You ripped your new shirt and you are going home to tell your parents.

• Someone told you you made a mistake.

• The team is being picked and you might be last.

• You are asked to try something you haven't tried before.

Teacher:

Spend brief periods in the role plays. (See Vol. I of roleplays) 2-3 minutes is usually enough time for getting the "action" you need. Don't push for a solution to the situation. Create the dilemma and process what the students are experiencing. Ask questions like:

What are the feelings you had as this role play was going on?

What did you notice you were saying to yourself as this happened?

Name three things that you could do when you are afraid

What are some other feelings you could feel instead of the ones you did?

The reasons we have fear is so we don't have to handle the world straight on. We behave out of our fear by masking our true self. We hope that when people see us they see our mask or our "act" instead of our self.

Forced Choice

Is your "act" more to (when you are afraid do you):

- giggle or cry

do you

- attack or withdraw

do you

- blame or hide

do you

- talk to yourself or try to avoid yourself

If you had to describe your behavior when you are afraid are you more:

- shakey or stoic

- deliberate or tentative

Inventories

- Things about others with which I scare myself the most

    Code · · · P = physical characteristics

    S = size

    M = mental things

    D = distance socially

    A = authority

    R = relationship

- Things in myself that are scary to me
- Fears I know I don't have
- Things in myself others may be afraid of

Fear

Rank order

- Which do you prefer to feel —

  ____ fear

  ____ guilt

  ____ sadness

  Let those who choose each of these gather in a small group to discuss their choice.

- What is the main reason you get afraid?

  ____ You don't know something.

  ____ You are faced with someone bigger than you.

  ____ You might get hurt.

  Write something in your journal about you and your choice.

  Get with one other person and share your thoughts about why you get afraid.

- Which would be more scary for you?

  ____ rock climbing

  ____ parachuting

  ____ hang gliding

  Group the students and have them discuss their choices.

Fear

- In your journal decide of whom you are more afraid —

  Parents because _____

  Peers because _____

  Police because _____

  Principal because _____

- Rank order the following — (most to least scary)

  _____ animals

  _____ ideas

  _____ other people

  _____ machines

  _____ that I won't be able to love

  _____ that people think I'm dumb

  _____ that my needs won't be met

  _____ that I'll not be able to say what I want

  _____ giving a speech

  _____ walking alone at night

  _____ meeting a new person

  _____ interviewing for a job

  Process in small groups.

Fear

Spectrums

On a wall in your classroom place the following numbers in this order:

−3 −2 −1 0 +1 +2 +3

−3	=	strongly disagree
−2	=	moderately disagree
−1	=	disagree
0	=	no stand — can't make a choice
+1	=	agree
+2	=	moderately agree
+3	=	strongly agree

Read the following to your class and have them line up in front of the number that most represents their position.

- People could live longer if they weren't afraid.

- Fear would go away if people would trust each other more.

- People are more afraid of people than ideas.

- People are more afraid of people than things.

- Bodies tell us about what fear is and what we think it will do.

- You can choose something other than fear when you are about to be afraid.

- Fear keeps one from responding to fear.

- One of my greatest fears is not being able to meet expectations of others.

Fear

- I'm often afraid.

- It's easy for me to discuss my fears.

- I mostly don't feel in charge of being afraid.

- Fear keeps me on my guard.

- Fear is good.

Brainstorm

- Ways to know a person is afraid

- How to rid this classroom of fears

- Major reasons why people get afraid

- How people cover up their fear

- All the things people are afraid of (Prioritize these in order to reach some group view of fears)

- Ways of resisting fear so we don't deal with it

Activities

☆

Breathing and Fear

Have students close their eyes and imagine something with which they scare themselves (the night, heights, etc.) As they are seeing and experiencing their fear focus their attention on their breathing by saying "listen to yourself breathe, is it short? fast? shallow? deep? Pay attention to your breathing and try to slow it down. You can do it by imagining the scale and lowering your breathing." After this have them look back at their fear with their new, deeper breathing. "Go back to experiencing your fear while you keep your breathing. Stay there for awhile." After about a minute have them slowly open their eyes and share what it was like to handle their fear this way.

Process questions you might ask:

• In what ways was your breathing affecting your fearing or vise versa?

• Think of a time when you can practice "breathing your fear."

• Write yourself a paragraph in your journal about this.

• What conclusions do you draw from this activity?

Guided Fantasy

• Close your eyes and get comfortable. Think of someone in your life that you let scare you. See them very clearly. What are they wearing? How tall are they? What do they hold in their hand? What does their voice sound like? I'm going to ask you to change them. Make them shorter. Have them hold a flower in their hand. Have them move away from you. Have the sun shine on their smile. Have them hold out a gift to you. How do you feel towards them now? Return to your place and slowly open your eyes.

Fear

- Close your eyes and count your breaths, taking each breath in a little further. Feel your body relax. Identify the thing in the world you are afraid of. It might be darkness, speed, bright lights, height, a person. Identify that thing and look at it in your mind's eye. See yourself seeing it. Slowly do a body scan to see where you most experience that fear. Start at the top of your head and go to your toes to find out where most of your "fear attention" goes. Go back to those places and shine the light of the sun on them so that they glow. Feel the warmth the sun produces. See yourself, your fear and the sun as forming a triangle. Watch how these interact. Go to the next part of your body and do the same thing. Watch your "fear attention" turn to warmth. Relax and slowly return to this room.

Journal Entries

- Write a letter to yourself exaggerating all the fears that you have. See all of them as sentences you say to yourself that are only made up of words.

- Find someone who is afraid of the same things as you are and write to them in your journal.

- List all the reasons why you should stay afraid of the things you are afraid of.

- List all the things you don't get to do because you are afraid.

- Starting with "dying" make a further list of what will happen to you if you start to be unafraid of your fears.

- When you catch yourself being afraid, act as a film director and rewrite the script.

Feelings

Introduction

"How do you feel?"

"I know exactly how you feel."

"She wears her feelings on her cuff."

We all have them — we all express them — we all experience them — we know what they are and yet feelings are for many people vague, hidden. People are in "therapy" to learn how to express them, many don't trust them and feelings are denied by many.

Why this dilemma over feelings? Is it because we are rugged American individualists who only show feelings in private? Is it because religious training requires trust in God and therefore no emotions? Is it because we haven't developed emotionally as other cultures have?

Purpose

- to learn to take responsibility for our own feelings

- to know the differences between thoughts and feelings

- to practice the expression of feelings

- to value feelings as an integral part of our existence

- to express self disclosure as growth-producing

Feelings

Definition

Get your students to define the word "feelings." Also facilitate them in the following:

Feelings are different from thoughts in that they
_____

Feelings and emotions are the same/different in that
_____

Feelings are _____

When I feel I _____

Discussion Starters

- If anyone feels anything she is responsible for the feeling.

- Feelings can hurt others.

- Feelings can't be trusted.

- Feelings are the way we perceive ourselves.

- When our feelings are settled we experience our highest consciousness.

- No two people have the same way of integrating what they perceive.

- The reality we derive from our perceptions is largely a creation of our own needs and expectations.

- Feelings are the truth.

- When a feeling is avoided, its painful effects are often prolonged and it becomes increasingly difficult to deal with it.

Feelings

- Sometimes the reason people feel bad is that they keep imitating their memories of themselves.

- When you feel angry or rejecting toward me, I can hurt myself by imagining that that's the only way you feel.

- When I learn to recognize and accept my own feelings, I become less vulnerable to other people's ideas about how I "should feel."

Journals

- Sometimes writing your feelings helps you express your feelings. Take some time each day to write to yourself about your feelings — about yourself.

- Make a list of feelings that you try to get rid of. After getting your list take one of them and with your eyes closed pay close attention to not getting rid of it but to holding it close to you.

- There are times when we have opposite feelings toward the same thing or person. Make your list of times when you could remember you hated/loved — a time you were happy/sad at the same time.

- Sometimes families have "acceptable" and "unacceptable" ways to feel. Take a look at your family and make your lists of unacceptable and acceptable feelings. Do you find any messages that you are being given about the good/bad feelings?

- Give the parts of your body voices. Write down what these parts say about feelings. What parts are sad, happy, angry, etc.

- Discover how you have temper tantrums.

Circletime

- A feeling I keep having

- A feeling I wish I would have more often

- It seems as though others have the feeling of _____ more than I do

- When I see someone experiencing a feeling and they don't know what to do with it, I usually _____

- A time when I behaved out of my feelings and everything turned out for me

- A time when I behaved out of my feelings and things turned out negative for me

- A time my feelings were so strong I didn't know what to do

- A feeling of mine I don't understand

- How I know when someone's feeling a certain way

- What I do with negative feelings

- What I do with negative feelings of others

- A joyous feeling I recall

Body Spectrums

- If people could change their feelings they would still be dissatisfied.

- Negative feelings are harmful.

- If people don't express feelings they will probably get sick.

- Feelings are more important than thoughts.

- Anxiety is the fear of hurt or loss.

- Hurt or loss leads to anger.

- Anger held for any length of time leads to guilt.

- Guilt, unrelieved, leads to depression.

- The best way to deal with bad feelings is to hide them.

- It is possible to change your feelings purposely.

Feelings

Inventories

• Things toward which I have negative feelings.

• Things toward which I have positive feelings.

• Things toward which I have ambivalent feelings.

• Things toward which I have neutral feelings.

• Things toward which I have no feelings.

CODE:

Have your students code in the following ways:

O =   often

S =   seldom

★ =   important

B =   you behave to change or keep the thing

A =   you are aware of your feelings when this thing happens or is present

Feelings

List as many things as you can that you . . . .

- *fear*

- are *sad about*

- are *angry about*

- are *joyful about*

Code:

    T —   you can touch the thing you have feelings about.

    O —   you have this feeling often.

    C —   you change the feeling when you have it.

    E —   you can express your feeling when you choose it.

    L —   you can let it go.

    G —   you feel guilty about the feeling.

    F —   you flow with the feeling.

Role Plays

- Two people are criticizing each other.

- A person gives you a compliment.

- You are asked to go out with someone.

- Your name appears in the school newspaper. Your friend is reading it to you.

- Someone tells you that if you don't change your attitude you're in for some rough times.

- You are being asked to go rock climbing. You have never done it before.

- Someone is making noise so that you are interrupted in what you are doing.

    (Have your students make up additional role plays)

Process:

The purpose of these role plays is to focus on feelings your students have in these situations. Ask them questions like:

    What kinds of feelings did you experience?

    What other feelings could you have had?

    What do you do with ambivalent feelings?

    How come some people have one feeling and others another feeling in the same situation?

Feelings

Rank order

• Which do you prefer doing?

> Screaming
>
> Crying
>
> Sulking

If you could only choose one, what would be the pros and cons of each?

• Which feels more like you?

Anger

Fear

Sadness

What would happen if you were more of one other?

• Prioritize the following as to which gives you the most joyful feeling:

__ skiing		__ swimming
__ skating		__ watching TV
__ dancing		__ eating
__ reading		__ traveling
__ writing		__ others (what?)

How often do you choose to do what you get joy from?

- Which do you find easiest to do?

  Cry in public

  Express your anger

  Do something you are scared to do

- Which loss is greatest for you?

  Loss of love

  Loss of control

  Loss of self-esteem

  Discuss the reasons for your choices with another person.

Brainstorm

- How to finish unfinished anger

- How to learn to choose feelings

- How our minds affect our feelings

- How laughing makes a person vulnerable

- Words people gave you about having or experiencing feelings

- How to make someone laugh

- How to use your depression to your advantage

- How to make sure someone understands your anger

- All the things people laugh about

Activities

☆

Feeling Auction —

Give each student $1000 for the sale of feelings. Make a long list of feelings. (List at least three feelings for each student.) Each student can "buy" three feelings maximum. Indicate to them that they are to study the feeling list, make their decision and proceed in the auction. Some students may save their $1000 for one feeling. What happens when only one gets the feeling? When several wanted it?

☆

Paying Attention

During the course of the day, stop to pay attention to what you are feeling. Don't only watch or listen to the strong feelings. Be aware of the subtle ones too. Notice that when you notice one feeling another one comes to take its place. Be aware of whether you are experiencing your feelings or what you remember your feelings to be. Are you thinking your feelings or feeling your feelings?

In a small group discuss the difference.

☆

Listen to the Room

The next time you walk into a room instead of beginning a conversation or greeting someone, pay close attention to what's going on and how you feel there. Use your senses. What is it about the room or each person that triggers the feelings in you?

☆

Reasons for Feelings

Sometimes people lose the essence of their feelings by having to give reasons for them to others. The next time someone asks you why you feel the way you do tell them gently "because that's the way I feel."

☆

Exaggerate — Slow down

Feelings come fast. You may see something and feel happy. Your choice of feelings are rapid. Choose some times when you could slow down and exaggerate your feelings. Feelings can be savored or examined by doing this.

☆

Prioritizing Feelings

List all the things you fear. Cut your list so you have each fear on one piece of paper. Shuffle your fears around until you have them listed from least to most feared. Now that you have your list you can begin a gradual disidentification with the ones you fear the least.

Close your eyes and visualize your fear, the place you experience it, the people involved in it. Move closer to the fear in your mind's eye. Notice what happens to your fear as you own it more as your own.

Feelings

☆

Breathing and Feeling

Sometimes when people are sad or afraid or happy or angry they forget to breathe. When you next experience one of these feelings remember to breathe deeply and notice what happens?

☆

Give it a Day

When someone gets angry at you, tell them you are not going to respond to them for a day. Tell them you want to think about what they said, not just respond out of defensiveness or guilt.

☆

Song

Write a song about feelings. Present it to your class

☆

Humor

Write a joke. Try it on some people. What makes the joke funny?

My Dreamer

Introduction

Each of us has a dreamer, an inner, visualizing self that operates, apparently outside of time, and sees what-could-be, before it beomes what-is. Not only are night-dreams, daydreams, hunches, fantasies and intuitions the products of this dreaming self, but much of what we would term our rational, waking experience. The dreamer is the source of all we create. In one sense, we are constantly "materializing" dream-stuff into physical existence. Einstein stated that "imagination is more important than knowledge." Two Nobel Prize winners dreamed the solutions to their problems. Indeed, the greatest scientific "breakthroughs" are always perceived, not so much through the intellect (which collects, sorts and categorizes the data in a more-or-less straight-line fashion), but through the intuition, which receives wholistically — outside of space and time — and arranges data into simultaneous gestalts of consciousness, the tapestried evidences of what we call "genius." While schools have tended to overlook or underplay other means of knowing than the cognitive-intellective mode, there is really no reason why the teacher of today cannot make appeal to the deeper, inner self of the student — the dreamer. In doing so, the teacher is truly educating for "life-out-there" beyond the classroom — where being *right* is often not so important as being *related.*

My Dreamer

Purposes

- To legitimize dreaming as an important, enjoyable, creative, therapeutic, necessary educational activity

- To enable the student to accept his/her 'dreamer' as a vital part of his/her being

- To practice and develop dream "skills" that the student will use all his/her life

- To dispel awe, fear, and needless misunderstanding about dreams and dying

- To enable each student to use dreams as a vital learning and decision-making resource

Definition

"Close your eyes for a moment, and purposely relax . . . let go of people and events around you . . . go to a place now, in your mind, where you'd really like to be . . . spend some moments there, look around, see, hear, smell, touch . . . . (pause 30 seconds) . . . now, come back here and open your eyes . . .

Open your journal and make notes on your dream. Write down — in paragraph or list form — as many details as you remember." (Allow 2 minutes.)

In the margin, write the emotions you felt about each aspect or event of the dream. For instance, you might have felt pleasant feelings at being back at a favorite place of yours — and then a little lonely if no one else was there, etc. Let's just brainstorm some feelings people might have experienced during this dream." (Take 8 or 10, encouraging a range. Allow 1 minute for noting feelings in journals.)

My Dreamer

Process the experience by saying:

"I've been calling what you did a *dream*. What are other names for it?" (Fantasy, daydream, wish, trip, fancy, image, mental excursion, etc. . . . Write these on a chart, and keep adding to the list of "kinds of dreaming" as you continue the unit.)

"What do you have to do (use) in order to dream?"

Develop the idea that, even if some of us are not conscious of the process, everyone has a 'dreamer' inside, who operates night and day. With the agreed-upon definition of dreams, dreaming and dreamer, have students list all the ways each has used her/his dreamer "already today." Planning what to wear, imagining the day, its schedule of projected events, the fantasy task, anticipating next class, etc.

Discussion Starters

• Find things can you see right now that weren't first 'dreamed up'?

• How are "progress" and "dreaming" related?

• Do dreams seem to come from inside you or outside you? Where *do* they come from?

• How many of you know you dream at night? How many remember your dreams?

• Think of a time you 'say' something in your mind, then brought it into being . . . Tell about it.

• How is dreaming related to vision, memory, imagination, creativity?

• Share a time when a "dream" you had happened.

Teacher: Guidelines for conducting the unit . . .

1. Accept the wide range of feelings, attitudes, beliefs, habits and behaviors with regard to dreams that our society reflects. Many children have never discussed dreams before. To do so, for any of us, means to share a deep and often mysterious part of us. The subject may be fraught with religious, mystical, or psychological significance for some. Some may believe they never dream. Some will insist on "interpreting" dreams.

2. Never attempt to interpret another's dream — even if asked to.

3. Maintain an attitude of objective investigation about the subject. Present students with all material you can find on the subject.

4. Never force anyone to discuss, share, take part. Maintain the 'pass' option.

5. Try always to connect (get students to connect) dreams and dreaming with feelings, thoughts and beliefs.

My Dreamer

Circletime

- My feelings, in general, about dreams

- A dream I remember

- A scary dream

- My belief about dreams

- A dream that surprised me

- A dream that seemed to predict the future

- Something I've heard said about dreams or dreaming

- Something I often dream about

- A pleasant dream

- A dream I don't understand

- A dream that told me something I should do

- A dream I have mixed feelings about

- What I think a certain dream of mine "means"

- A place I go (person I see, event or object that repeats itself) in my dreams

- My feelings about myself as a dreamer

- Something I think is true about dreams or dreaming

- A thought I have about my dreams

Journal Entries

- Attitude Spectrum:

-     -   0   +   +
-                       +

  Place an X on the line to show where your feelings are,
  from very bad, to very good, about dreams in general.
  Write a statement about where your X went.

- Dream log

  Begin keeping a log of your dreams. This record
  should include date, general account of the dream,
  feelings you recall associated with the dream events, and
  any conclusions. Do this for one month. What patterns do
  you note?

- Draw a dream

  Illustrate a dream landscape or setting. See how many
  remembered details you can include.

Roleplays

- Have small groups of students plan short enactments of sharable dreams. Encourage the construction of props, masks and costumes to depict symbols.

- Do short fun skits entitled:

Nightmare	Monster
The Message	Run!
Mystery	The Ideal Dream
Flying	The Falling Dream
Two of Me	The Slow-Motion Dream
Lover	. . . etc.

- Acting out a Dream:

  Have students work in groups of 4. One person tells a dream, and assigns people (or they choose) to play other parts of the dream. The person then talks, in the first person, about *feeling toward* each other symbol. Without "redoing" the dream drama, talk in the present, using I, about dream reactions. Switch parts; take turns.

Activities

☆

Teacher: Once a week or so, guide the class in the dreamwork process that deals with their night dreams. They can use private entries in their journals or tell partners or share in a small support group.

Along the way, you can "teach the class to night dream" (something each person does already). Begin by covering these points:

1. Everyone dreams, every night. Without the functional processes provided by dreaming, we would take little or no refreshment from sleep (which is mere *inactivity*, and *can* be stressful). People who are kept, in lab experiments, from dreaming develop symptoms of stress, nervousness, loss of appetite, hostility — and even get sick. Dreaming is not only normal but vital to effective human functioning.

2. The real "work" of the dream is thus done *during* the event itself. The "dreamwork" activities are designed to increase our waking effectiveness — for we can teach ourselves much through work on dreams. For a dream is, in one sense, a visual, symbolic message *from* the self *to* the self, and can promote self-understanding, health and effectiveness at intuitive levels.

3. Though you may not recall your dreams, you can train yourself to do so quite easily. Remember that the Dreamer in each of us is not the same as the Sayer, and that, while words or ideas used in this context may not seem to "make sense" (and childrens' belief systems may cause them to resist being less "sensible"), it is possible and safe to know that you are 100% in charge of the decisions of your mind. Follow these guidelines as an experiment . . . . .

A.   When you go to bed, *just* before going to sleep (this is to be clearly recognized as the "twilight" — a hovering zone between wakefulness and sleep), suggest to yourself "I will remember my dream." Repeat this, with belief and intention, to yourself *as you fall asleep. Expect* to waken refreshed, and in full recall.

B.   It may take several successive nights to accomplish this, but expect it on the first, and on each night thereafter.

C.   Keep a notebook and pen by the bed, on which to make notes on the dream (brief notes if you wake in the night after a dream, and full accounts the next day, again on the initial-exercise model).

D.   You can train yourself, in a similar manner by self-suggestion, to *choose* a dream — to dream solutions and viewpoints on any issue or subject.

E.   Always "own" the dream, and each part of it, for your own. You *composed* the dream, so that you could watch and learn from it. (This is as if our Dreamer has a sort of goal-orientation, which it does not; it could not help dreaming if it tried!)

☆

Mandalas

Have each student draw a circle and construct a mandala, or "whole picture" of a dream, by placing symbols in a design relation to one another and the center point so that, somehow, the resulting mandala shows the dream as a gestalt or whole thing.

☆

Our Dreams

Any medium may be used — either two or 3-dimensional — a bulletin-board, *class collage* with this title, following a Circletime on the topic in which students share "a dream of mine for the future."

Have class devise other means of sharing their hopes, fantasies, wishes, and future plans.

☆

Diads

Seat students with partners of their choice. One student in each diad, on your direction, close eyes, relax, and purposely projects self into a night dream or other dream. This student is to "become" him/herself in the dream — or someone or something else in the dream — and talk out loud to the partner as if the dream event is happening in the present. ("Now the road I've been walking on is becoming filled with leaves, and the buildings are changing . . . ," etc.).

After 2-3 minutes, switch partners. Stop the activity, and have partners share their awareness and their feelings. Then open up a short, total-group discussion.

This activity can be repeated several different times with effectiveness. The more the child places him/herself with trust into the dream event — awake or asleep — the more confidence and trust in the Dreamer develops.

☆

Talking to a Mirror

Assign students to do this at home. Get alone and undisturbed for ten minutes with a mirror. Talk to the person in it, fully as if it were someone else. Talk back, as that person. Discuss whatever issues come to mind. Purposely, for the last five minutes or so, see if you can "get lost" as to which person "you are." How is this like dreaming? Why do people say, seriously, "talk to yourself in the mirror about that?"

☆

Ask A Medium To Class

Get parents' permission in writing, explaining study objectives; and that you do not plan to have the visitor "perform" (such as conducting a seance), but discuss her work with the class and answer questions. (Have several questions related to dreams and dreaming prepared ahead.)

Follow this up with a visit from a psychiatrist or psychologist, who can tell the class how dreams are used in therapy.

Playing

Introduction

Play comes naturally to children. Most children these days are surrounded by gadgetry designed to stimulate play and playfulness. Even though there are times when little is left to the imagination, most children take the mass produced play things and toys and transform them into the dreams and wishes of their imaginations and fantasies.

When children grow up, they seem to lose their playfulness and sense of creativity and delight to get more serious and reasonable. The logical overpowers the illogical and the rational overpowers the irrational. In each adult the remnant of the "child" persists, covered and encrusted — but still there. In safe times the "child" in each of us "plays" to exhaustion. When we adults really hurt the child cries. When surprises are surprises the child glees. When problems are solved intuitively the child says with cocky smile — "I told you so."

Purpose

- to create the attitude where permission to play is easy

- to accept all of life as playing not working

- to design ways to free up the "child" to play

- to experience the total involvement of playfulness

Definition

- Make a list of examples of playing —

- From your list make categories on the "kinds" of playing there are.

- Find out how many category — connectors there are in the contributions to help define what "play" may mean to people.

Discussion Starters

- How is war like playing?

- How is playing like war?

- What if people only played to get exercise?

- The importance of playing in a person's life

- What does a person have to do to really be involved in play activity?

- How do animals play? How is their play like people-play?

- How "shoulds" and "oughts" get in the way of playing

- The differences between play and work

- The difference bewteen spontaneous play and planned play

- There was no longer enough work for everyone and we had to spend our time in play and leisure activities

- How our technology helps or hinders play

Circletime

- Games I must enjoy

- When I play I experience myself feeling _____

- A time when play is most rewarding

- Things I say to myself when I'm playing

- What I've noticed about my skill in playing

- Describe a time when you forgot what was going on because you were playing so hard.

- A game I'd like to learn

- How I experience pain when I play

- Someone offered to include me in their play.

Role Play

Some people play games that can be destructive to relationships. These are usually interaction games where the people in the interaction are playing one of three roles and usually switching roles in the middle of the interaction. The roles are victim — persecutor — rescuer. The names of the games are

_____

    If it weren't for _____
    Ain't it awful?
    Now I've got you, you son of a bitch
    Blemish (I'm better than you)
    Wooden leg (I have no power)
    Kick me (I deserve it)
    Poor me

There are two roles included in each game. Have some students plan the role play, play it in front of the class, and process it by using the following:

• When were there times when people changed roles in the interaction?

• Describe the feelings and behaviors which were going between the players.

• In your journal list the people with whom you play these games. Can you break it?

Inventories

• Things I think are important for playing

• Ways I see myself being more playful

• All the ways I play

• Ideal conditions for me to play

• "Players" I admire

• My goals in play

• My needs in play

• How I play "at work"

• My "playmates"

Coding suggestions:

M	—	male	MO	—	money
F	—	female	E	—	exercise
A	—	active	AT	—	attention
P	—	passive	PO	—	power

Forced Choice

Would you rather —

•   be in charge of scheduling a play period OR
    participate in something someone else planned

Playing has more to do with —

•   endurance
        than
    dexterity

•   courage
        than
    knowledge

•   curiosity
        than
    strength

•   the urge to be first
        than
    exercise

Rank Order

•   I have the most fun —

    __   flying a kite

    __   baking a cake

    __   building a model

    __   reading a book

    __   shooting a basketball

    __   solving a problem

Playing

___ riding in a car

___ cleaning my room

___ swimming

___ playing a board game

___ playing cards

___ playing baseball

- Things I most don't want to hear when I'm playing —

  ___ you're doing it wrong

  ___ let me show you

  ___ time to quit

  ___ you'll never be able to do it

  ___ just keep trying

  ___ you go last

- What part of me seems to be the most involved when I play —

  ___ hands

  ___ eyes

  ___ feet

  ___ brain

  ___ legs

  ___ arms

  ___ other (what? _____)

Playing

Brainstorm

- How to make our classroom more fun

- How to teach others to be more playful

- How to make things which seem to be drudgery into play

- How to feel free enough to be spontaneous

- Things that hinder people from being playful

- "Permissions" people need to play

    __ from self?
    __ from others?
    __ from environment?

Whips

- I like to play _____ .

- I learned _____ when I played _____ .

- I'm afraid to play _____ .

- I learned to play _____ .

- I was surprised I enjoyed playing _____ .

- I wish I knew how to play _____ .

- I imagine myself as a great player of _____ .

- Card games I like are _____ .

- I'm aware of _____ when I play _____ .

Guided Fantasy

Close your eyes, relax, see yourself at your present age. Focus in on how you play at your age. Are you alone or in groups? Are you spontaneous or planning your play? What parts of your body are most involved in your playing?

Gradually go back through your years. See yourself at age 12, at 10, at 8, at 6, as a pre-schooler, and notice how you played at those times (Teacher: you may want to spread this activity over a few days. Give students sufficient time to re-experience their playing selves).

After this age span have students write in their journals describing in as fullest detail as possible the kind of player they were. After they have gathered this data ask them to respond to the following:

- How your playing partners have changed

- What of your earlier playing patterns still remain as part of you

- Awareness you get through these guided fantasies about yourself

- Changes you want to make in your playing self

Playing

Activities

☆

Imagination

(Teacher: Imagination skills generally stimulate creativity in students. As traditional education encourages pretending, day-dreaming and imagination students will discover new varieties in perceiving the world.)

Have your students close their eyes and relax. Ask them to imagine that they are the following people. Give them at least a minute for each role.

- "You are now becoming a baker . . . . Watch what you do, watch the people who are around you, notice what makes you happy or sad."

- "You are now going to change into a circus clown . . . ."

- "You are now going to become an athlete . . . ."

- "You are now becoming a person who does risky things . . . ."

- "You are now becoming a public person — someone everyone knows . . . ."

Process:

Discuss ways we can "Play" with fear or risks. How were feelings of playing present for you?

Was it more fun doing the thing or being watched doing the thing?

In your journal write something you learned about yourself.

☆

Clowns

For this activity either invite a clown or study the art of clowning as a class project. After you have the information you need try some of the following:

• Make yourself up as clowns and spend the day or part of the day being clowns in your school or town. Study your reactions and the reactions of others. Notice what people do with you or with your clown. Do they know how to "play with you" or is their "play" more observation? What "permission" do people need to play?

• Go to a local supermarket as a clown but don't act like a clown, act like you would usually. What do people do with the discrepancy they experience? Compare their reactions with the group above.

• See whether you can get into a theater as a clown. What are some of the remarks you hear?

• Plan a clown day for your school where you teach others how to be clowns. Try to isolate the kinds of skills you would want others to master.

Process:

How do you "unbecome yourself" when you become a clown?

How are you still yourself when you become the clown?

What kinds of feelings do you have when you stop being the clown?

Imagine you could be the clown always. What would that be like?

Being a clown is like being _____ .

As a clown I realized that others _____ .

☆

Dress-up-Masquerade

"Dress-up" is something we played when we were young. If you go into a K-3 classroom you will see youngsters "dressing-up" to pretend a role. The game served the function of enabling us to act out part of a personality we had or wish we had. The need to do some version of the game is incorporated into the life of each of us. How do we express and fulfill this need? Culturally we set aside Halloween, when it's all right to dress up "out front." Within sub-cultures "dress-up" goes on subtly and with overtones of refined ritual. Have your students experience some of the following:

• Have a discussion on the ways in which young people dress-up. How do changing fashions indicate the dress-up that goes on in our culture?

• Plan a dress-up day for your class. Do it in such a way that students help each other with the decision of what they will wear, who they want to represent, how they will get their costumes. Require originality. Avoid the typical Halloween costumes like bum and witch. Encourage historical figures, literary personalities, movie stars, athletes, entertainers, people in local and national news. Consider using make-up.

The purpose for the dress-up is to try on and to play with the personality of the one each is emulating. Afterwards have them look carefully at what it was like to *be* that other person. Find ways to have other than the class respond to them. The public adds the dimension of being looked at. The drama is complete with an audience. Set this as a major objective, so the exercise becomes more than a masquerade, more than a roleplay. Plan with students to make at least a portion of the event "living theater" — a spontaneous watching-yourself-be-someone-else.

☆

Street Theater

In some large cities or university towns the street minstrel is returning. Encourage your class to do some of the following:

- Create a short play that speaks to an issue of the day. Keep it about three minutes. Walk through your town or your part of the city stopping periodically to do your play. If you have handbills they can be handed to people so they understand what you're doing. If you have two or three short plays you can offer variety. Try to include music with guitar or horns to attract attention. In dramatizing issues in this way students participate in ancient art.

- Spend the day in a singing presentation which strolls your streets. In small groups with guitar accompaniment present your town with some oldies and newies. Encourage folks to sing along.

- For smaller children, create a marionette show. Take your act into other classes; or get some space at a near-by mall on a Saturday afternoon and provide entertainment and involvement for children.

Sexism

Introduction

Sexism is a game of victim. When people decide they have been discriminated against for whatever reason they can easily feel victimized. But since all feelings originate within each person the only "un-phoney" words a person can say are "I am victimizing myself with this treatment by you." That's different from "you're victimizing me." The victim role comes from one who is feeling insecure, unconfident, doubtful and fearful. (The same is true of the persecutor or rescuer roles.) So if one is feeling discriminated on the basis of sex one is really saying "I doubt my sex roll" or "I'm not confident as a man/woman."

Purposes:

- to create environments where students can feel more confident as a man or woman

- to have each person more fully crasp how discrimination functions for or against them

- to have students examine how they "use" their sex in positive or negative ways

Definition

As a class comes up with a definition of sexism or sex role discrimination keep from focusing on discrimination "done to" one sex only. Guide the discussion so that sex-role stereotyping is seen as a *game* ("dance") that cannot be played alone.

Sources you might use are:

> Books on the subject of "Liberation"
> Quotes from magazine articles
> Interviews of people in your community

Discussion Starters

- What would happen if we got rid of the masculine and feminine pronouns in our written and spoken language? How would you do it?

- The unisex look is more and more popular. What is this saying about sex role discrimination?

- Many women are seeking after the traditional male roles. Why aren't men seeking traditional female roles?

- If we have working mothers should we also have house husbands?

- What do parents do to lead their children into traditional roles?

- React to the following quote —

  "We have to make ourselves not as a projected ideal, but out of the shapes of the here and now. The barriers which confront us are real, not merely the conjurings of our imagination."
  - Shela Rowbotham

- What would it be like if we got rid of sex role types?

- People have both masculine and feminine qualities in them at the same time.

- How we view sex is how we view the world and how we view the world is how we view sex.

- I bring to my sexual contact the same vision and consciousness I bring to any other activity.

Sexism

- People don't have discrimination done to them, they perceive discrimination and therefore they are.

- How I think society dictates sex roles and how I can change in that society.

Circletime

- A time being a man/woman was disadvantage/advantage

- I noticed I was treated unfairly because of my sex

- If I could do one thing as a woman I would

- If I could do one thing as a man I would

- I like me male/female because

- I make myself more aware of my sex because _____

- How I experience my femaleness

- How I experience my maleness

- A time I changed my feelings about sex roles and found a new way to look at things.

- I made a decision out of a consciousness of my sex

- A positive thought that I think about my sex

Rank Order

Things about myself that I value from most to least

____ gentleness

____ assertiveness

____ open mindedness

Sexism

____ strength

____ concern

____ wisdom

____ skills

How I most express my sexness

____ showing off

____ being strong

____ helping others

____ being competent

____ being weak

____ being flirtatous

____ arguing

Where you think sex role stereotyping comes from

____ from institutions

____ from within the person

____ from families

____ from culture

Journals

- Write a letter to the female half of you about your maleness.

- Write a letter to the male half of you about your femaleness.

- The role of male or female is both a cultural and hereditary thing. Write to yourself which ways your family has valued femaleness and maleness.

- The things you like most about your sex.

- Conduct an interview with yourself and answer the following questions:

  If you could be a male/female for one day what would you do?

  How do you most show your care for a person of the opposite sex — same sex? Why the difference, or why the same?

  What are the things you should or should not do as a man or woman? Make a list and then examine very closely why you should or shouldn't do each of them.

- Try to remember the times you say to yourself: "If you loved me you would _____ ." Each time you do you are not experiencing all you could.

- List the sex things over which you have some curiosity. Who will give you the answers?

Inventories

- Make a list of the things that you do as part of your role as a son or daughter in your home.

Code:

C — Cooking

CL — Cleaning

O — Outside work

M — Manual labor

T — Thinking task (problem solving)

MO — involves money

R — involves taking responsibility

I — You receive some kind of instruction before you do this.

- Make a list of advice you have received from adults.

Code:

M — has to do with money

R — has to do with taking responsibility

RE — has to do with relationships with others

H — has to do with being healthy

A — has to do with assisting others

F — has to do with being fair

G — has to do with being gentle

AG — has to do with being aggressive

E — has to do with your education

Role Plays

- Your name is Laura and you know how to pitch quite well. Try to get on the school team.

    Laura and coach interact
    Coach and players interact

- Your teacher has suggested the class go on an all day picnic. The organizing committee is all girls.

    Boy and girl interact
    Boy and teacher interact

- You are a boy and you want to learn to knit. A girl who knows how is showing you.
  (If it is possible to actually do this — better yet!)

- Play the part of a woman astronaut
                a woman weightlifter
                a woman pilot

Body Spectrums

- Women should decide what is woman and men should decide what is man

- Girls are more social than boys

- Girls are more suggestible than boys

- Boys have a higher self-esteem

- Girls are better at rote learning and simple repetitive tasks, boys at tasks that require higher-level cognitive processing

- Boys are more analytic

- Girls are more affected by heredity, boys by environment

- Girls lack achievement motivation

- Girls are auditory, boys visual

  (The previous eight have no basis in research)

- Girls have greater verbal ability than boys

- Boys excel in math ability

- Males are more aggressive than females

  (The previous three have some basis in research)

Activities

☆

Career Guidance

Go into your guidance office and find brochures which describe jobs available to H. S. graduates. Notice if there is any exclusion by sex that is there. Are both men and women encouraged to apply for all jobs?

☆

ERA

At the time of this writing the Equal Rights Amendment had not been ratified by the sufficient number of states to change the Constitution. Plan to spend some time interviewing people on their position on ERA. Try to judge whether people are speaking out of knowledge of the change or out of an emotional bias or fear.

☆

Woman Professionals

Check if you know —
__ woman doctor
__ woman lawyer
__ woman dentist
__ woman veterinarian
__ man nurse
__ man telephone operator
__ man secretary
__ woman barber
__ woman plumber
__ woman electrician
__ woman road worker
__ man maid

Sexism

☆

Changing Words

Change the following to be non-discriminating

insurance man

middleman

workman

fireman

watchman

cameraman

statesman

men in the field

men of God

men of science

salesman

businessman

forefathers

fatherland

founding fathers

Don't send a boy to do a man's job

Give a kid a job and help mold a man

☆

Male — Female — Both

Check male, female or both after each of the following words indicating that these characteristics are present and admirable in one sex or both.

	Male	Female	Both
Emotionally stable			
Sexually attractive			
Flirtatious			
Interested in Religion			
Economically Sufficient			
Professionally Ambitious			
Physically Strong			
Intellectually Quick			
Willing to take a risk			
Ready to Argue Easily			
Eloquent Speaker			
Passive			

Process:

      Why do you mark some M, some F some B?
      Discuss when these generalizations treat people unfairly.
      What feelings attend each description for you?

☆

Occupations

Brainstorm a list of occupations. Have each student mark each occupation with M — F — or B (male, female or both). See whether obvious sexism attitudes emerge from their markings. Discuss which professions can not be done by both and why.

☆

Words

Create alternatives for the following:

Mankind

Primitive Man

Man's Achievements

If a man drove 50 miles . . .

The best man for the job

Man-made

Grow to Manhood

☆

Sex Biased Words

Change the following to terms of dignity:

the weaker sex

the distaff side

girls or ladies (adult)

girl (I'll have my girl-secretary do that)

lady-used as a modifier

the little woman

the better half

sweet young thing

sweet young lady

career girl

Sexism

☆

Charades

Have a boy and girl act out an occupation written on a slip of paper. Slips are pulled from a hat at random. (Be sure to mix occupations traditionally held by men and woman.)

☆

Play "To Tell the Truth" having females and males playing mixed roles.

☆

Guided Fantasy

Close your eyes and take a few deep breathes to relax yourself. Find yourself in a quiet, peaceful, meadow. The sun is shining brightly and you see beautiful flowers, some birds and small animals. In front of you is a rose bush with many blooming flowers on it. To one side you see a bud about to open. Watch it very carefully as it opens. When it does you will see something that has to do with your life. Watch and listen . . . . (pause 30 seconds) Take one last look at your rose and when you feel comfortable open your eyes.

Take your journals and record your experience. (In about 4 minutes have your class share with another person and then anyone who wishes to share publicly.)

Taking Responsibility

Introduction

If there is one objective on which virtually all parents and educators agree as worthy of pursuing in school it is the development of self-responsibility in children. How do you "teach" someone responsibility? As with all skills, understandings, and anything that's learned, you can't *teach* anyone anything. What you *can* do is to be significantly present and to arrange things in such a way as to promote and encourage learning of the desired things by the child. When the "desired thing" is responsibility, most of us are stumped. In a world where there are few models for self-reliance, and where institutions, machines and others are viewed as robbers of a person's vital sense of responsibility for her/his own life, decisions, and welfare, most of us are too busy grasping for our own sense of identity and determinism to know how to help anyone else grow in this area.

We wish that kids would "be responsible," but we often are uncomfortable if they truly act that way — that is, act as if they are in charge of their own lives. Many of the ways we have of being with students, if they are examined carefully, are subtle means of perpetuating the psychological games of playing the Victim, or Naming and Blaming the Persecutor. (All of these games, which have many versions, are merely invitations to unload responsibility for our states of experiencing the world onto others!) Do we fully believe that in the end, each student is 100% responsible for what happens to her of him? — that, at the closing moments of that life, that person will not be able to honestly blame or place responsibility on others, even minutely, for any of the decisions and behaviors that have composed that life and brought meaning and value to it? The answer each of us makes to this question is of vital importance, for we will always act toward students out of our own structuring and defining of *what is real* — out of the representation of the world of others that we construct. If we see kids as victims, we'll rescue (parent). If we see them as responsible, we'll treat them that way (adult).

Purposes

- to aid each student in assuming full responsibility for his/her own experience (thoughts, feelings, perceptions, values, behavior), and not giving it away (playing Victim)

- to aid each student in attributing to others full responsibility for their experience, and not taking it away (playing Rescuer or Persecutor)

Definition

Note the words "response" and "able" in the word responsible. Play around as a group with ways to define the word using definitions and meaning combinations of these two smaller words. Check the dictionary. Have students share "I'm responsible when I . . ." in a whip. (Important: Guide the group into a discussion that contrasts the concepts of *fault* and *cause.* That is, help them to see that there is little or no productivity in taking up the question of "Who's responsible?" by attempting to place blame or fault (game of Who's Wrong); but great productivity in finding the origin of *cause* in a person's experience. Thus, each child comes to see that "Who's responsible?" always means "Who is at cause?" or "Who *owns* this (item, behavior, event, outcome?") Reinforce this concept of *ownership* of responsibility by beginning each day or period with questions like, "Who's responsible for the windows being open? (teacher) for the books being open? (students) for the room being swept? (custodian) etc." Continue throughout the unit, and in all your interactions with students, to follow the Rules of Responsibility (see activities) yourself. Be objective, descriptive, and *blame-free.*

· Discussion Starters

• Present the following assumptions for discussion:

1. Each of us is 100 % responsible.

2. No one can "do it to" (victimize) another, without that other's cooperation.

3. No one needs taking-care-of.

4. You only help me if I need you less after you've helped.

Do not defend any of these statements, but merely *reflect* the statements students make ("So you think . . . ;" "You disagree because it seems to you . . ." etc.).

• What sort of relationship develops if each person in it assumes 100 % for it? 50%?

• Place one or more of the following on the board each day and invite "I" statements about it. Reflect each.

— Nothing is "too" anything.

— You can't get hurt, really.

— Power is both a thing and an unthing; it is there for you if you take it, and it is there for others if you give it away.

— It doesn't matter.

• When do you *like* taking responsibility for yourself? When don't you? (Brainstorm lists; no agreement necessary)

- What is the difference, if any, between . . .

  "It's my (your) fault. I'm (you're) to blame." . . . and . . .

  "It's my (your) responsibility."

  What feelings emerge? what relationship (with self or other) sets up each time?

- What ways do we use to get others to take responsibility for us?

- Suppose you are "marooned" somewhere with a person. Would you rather the person be one who takes responsibility, or one who doesn't? Why?

Circletime

- A time I took responsibility that was mine

- A time I didn't take responsibility that was mine

- A way I have of assuming responsibility for myself

- A way I have of copping out (giving up responsibility for myself)

- A way I have of letting others be responsible

- A way I have of taking others' responsibility away from them

- A time I feel responsible

- A time I don't feel responsible

- How (when, with whom) I play Blame Games

- I talked my way out of it

Taking Responsibility

- The kind of person it's hard for me to feel responsible around

- A time I "rescue"

- What responsibility means to me

- Someone got me to take responsibility for them

- I spoke up when it was hard to

- I kept quiet when it was easier to

- A time I know I'm (knew I was) alone and responsible

- Why taking responsibility is hard for (easy for me)

- An "irresponsible" wish of mine

Here are some additional Circletime topics which are specifically aimed at having students experience their responsibility, or ownership, for what is theirs. At the beginning of each of these sessions, reinforce the idea that, while the "pass" option is in effect and no one has to talk, each person is to simply experience what emerges into his or her awareness as the task is contemplated. The topics are such that the real task for those who speak is to share openly, without some cover-up statements or wordings or behaviors that deny responsibility.

- I stole something

- The part of my body I admire

- Something I can do very well

- I didn't tell the truth

- Something I'm not too proud of

- A fear of mine

Process each session in terms of *feelings and motives* that emerged. How does your experience *here and now* relate to the subject of responsibility?

Journals

- Write ten "I can't . . ." statements. Now go back and reread each statement as an "I won't . . ." Who is responsible?

- Complete the following and make the suggested changes afterwards:

  1. I want to _____ but _____. (Change *but* to *and*)

  2. It bugs me when _____. It feels good to _____. I don't like it when _____. (Change *it* to *I* or *me*.)

  3. They won't let me _____. (Change *they* to *I*.)

  4. _____ makes me feel _____. (Change *I* make me feel _____ *with* _____.)

  Suggest a contract with a partner, to watch and give each other feedback on ways we can change our everyday language so as to tell the truth — i.e. assume responsibility that is ours fully. Each of the above entries, like the first, could be an entire inventory or list, one for each day in the journal. (Refer to the Phony Words Strategy in the How-to-Section for more on this.)

- Rank Order: I'd rather . . .

  __ Take responsibility for (take care of) another person

  __ Take responsiblity for (take care of) myself only

  __ Be taken care of by another

- My favorite roles

  __ victim

  __ persecutor

  __ rescuer

  __ none of the above

Inventories

- Ways I take responsibility

- Ways I don't

- Ways I get others to "rescue" me

- Ways I "rescue" others (Code: reward for each)

- Five hardest things for me to be self-responsible about (Code: reason for each; rank order; rewards, etc.)

- Five easiest things for me to be self-responsible about

- My "rescuers" (rank-order list)

- Things I say to myself when I'm "on the spot"

- Things I say to myself when I have to make a tough decision (Code 2 above with "Big Me" or "Little Me")

- Ways I "make people wrong"

- Ways I "make people right"

- Ten ways I could stop "copping out"
  (Code: Rank-order easiest to hardest; first thing I could see myself signing a contract to do; thing in each "cop-out" behavior that I want and would have to give up, etc.)

- Ways I play Victim (ask others to be responsible for me)

- Ways I play Rescuer (take other's responsibility away from them)

- People I tend to blame, and for what

- List of twenty VIP's (very important people to me)
  (Code: with R for "responsible," I for "irresponsible," L for "like me," U for "unlike me")

- Ten ways I've taken responsibility for myself today

- Five ways I haven't taken responsibility for myself today

- Ways I cop out, or shirk responsibility

- Hard things for me to do or say
  (Any of the above lists may be coded as you prefer. Suggestions: M for mother, F for father, O for often, S for seldom, plus-sign for positive feelings, minus for negative, R for risk, D for danger, V for victim, R for rescuer, P for persecutor,etc.)

Have each student write one sentence or paragraph beginning "My favorite way of getting others to take care of me . . . ;" and another beginning "My way of responding when someone wants to be taken-care-of . . ." Have students choose partners, create brief (one-minute) roleplays using the data, and present to the class. Discuss each roleplay in terms of the kinds of relationship, feelings, etc. that sets up.

Roleplays

Place each of the following on an index card. Have volunteers choose a card and a person or persons from the class with whom to plan and present the roleplay. Do one or two roleplays a day. Process each with the audience (class) afterwards, in terms of (a) what you saw happening; (b) brainstorm of appropriate titles; (c) where you see yourself in the roleplay.

1. *I Can't:* A is telling B all the things A can't do, complaining, commiserating. B says, "you know, you sound as if you can't do *any*thing!" A: "I CAN'T!" B: "you can do one thing." A: "Oh yeah? What's that?" B: "You can sure CAN'T!"

2. *Yeh-But:* A "victim" is surrounded by 3 or 4 friends who keep listening to how awful everything is about V's problem. Each person tries to suggest a solution or a way of dealing with the situation. V keeps responding with "Yeh-buts" (i.e., "I tried that and it didn't work . . . That's no good because . . . yeh but you're forgetting about . . ."). It's evident that V enjoys his role, won't give it up for anything.

3. *Boy Meets Girl:* Boy: "You turn me on." Girl: "How?" Boy: Oh, I dunno — the way you look." Girl: "You like the way I look." Boy: "Yeah." Girl: "Then, that's what *you're* doing." Boy: "Okay, then I'll say it the right way." Girl: "Go ahead." Boy: "I turn *myself* on looking at you." Girl: "I *like* it!"

4. *Before-and-Afters:* These are scenes that are presented twice, with a "new twist" the second time around.

    a. Look-what-you-made-me-do reaction to an accident, as against Look-what-happened-we-need, etc.

    b. Sorry-sorry-sorry (reaction of a person who keeps spilling things, messing up, bumping into people, etc.); as against doing it once and stopping it.

c. If-it-weren't-for-me (Rescuer game), as against being glad other person helped is now on her own.

d. *The fight:* Two friends are quarreling over something that happened and whose fault it was, who started it, etc. In second version, quarrel starts, as before. But friends decide the matter of fault-finding is dumb, and they begin to deal with what-are-you-going-to-do and what-am-I-going-to-do-next-time.

5. *Alter Ego:* This roleplay takes 3 people. A plays a person who obviously has some irritating qualities (complaining, bugging the other person with questions or suggestions, scratching or picking teeth, etc.) B is an associate of A's and a "reactor" to the irritating traits (acting disgusted, moving away, discounting other, etc.). C is another associate, who acts in a friendly way toward the irritator. A leaves, whereupon the other 2 converse. B: "What a turkey, huh?" C: "Who, Joe?" (B lists all A's faults, C listens, doesn't agree or disagree. B keeps on criticizing.) Finally, C says: "What is it about A that pushes *your* button?" B: "What do you mean?" C: "I think you must be *scared* of something." B: "Who, ME? Scared? Scared of WHAT?" C: "*I* don't know." (C leaves). B thinks to self: "*Scared.* Hm." (Audience brainstorms possible fears behind B's upset).

6. *Try-on:* Two friends are conversing. A is telling B about his father's requiring him to do chores. A says: "He probably thinks I'm *scared* of him or something. (Looks at B.) I'm *not* scared of him. I'm not scared of him one little BIT!" (Lot's of energy in the denial.) B: "Hey, try something for me, will you?" A: "What?" B: "Just say: 'I'm really scared of my father.' " A: (defiant, outraged) "That's not *true!*" B: "Just try it *on.*" A: "No *way. I'm* not going to say something that isn't true." (Follow this skit up with a discussion on taking responsibility for feelings, to oneself. Discuss the advisability of "try-ons.")

Forced Choice

Would you rather . . .

- Take care of OR be taken care of?

- Make a decision OR put if off?

- Be alone OR with others?

- Complain OR endure in silence?

- Help OR be helped?

- Lead OR follow?

- Rely on OR be relied on?

- Take the blame OR give the blame?

- Trust others OR mistrust them?

- Save your own life OR die saving another's?

- Have an experience OR tell about it?

Which is most attractive to you? (Go with the first thing you feel, gut level)

- A person in trouble, whom you could help OR a person in trouble, who could help him/herself?

- Someone who needs you OR someone who's bothering you?

- A person being right about something OR a person being wrong about something?

- Experiencing OR understanding?

- Giving responsibility OR taking responsibility?

- A "victim" OR a "rescuer?"

- Seeing myself as being a certain way OR being seen by others as being a certain way?

Rank Order

- ___ duty
  ___ challenge
  ___ responsibility

- ___ persecutor
  ___ rescuer
  ___ victim

- ___ can
  ___ can't
  ___ don't know

- ___ giving up
  ___ trying hard
  ___ letting-go
  ___ doing my best
  ___ seeing what happens
  ___ looking good
  ___ succeeding

Spectrums

Take a stand, on a spectrum of "least comfortable" (minus − 5) to "most comfortable" (Plus + 5), on each of the following:

- making decisions for myself

- taking care of others

- saying no to people

- confronting someone

- being a follower

- handing out orders

- being blamed for something you didn't do

Take a stand, on a spectrum of minus 5 (disagree strongly) to plus 5 (agree strongly), on each:

- people can be trusted

- being right always works

- everyone already knows everything

- things are bad

- people can't "do it" to you unless you let them

- I often cop out

- the most important thing is being fair

- you can't really get hurt

Brainstorms

(As with personal inventories, set time limits or quotas, ("2 minutes," "ten ways," etc.) and push for volume.)

• aspects of a future when every person acts 100% responsible

• reasons we blame each other

• things Big-Me (part of each person that takes charge, is not afraid, knows already) says (Example: "I can")

• things Little-Me (scared part that puts on act in order to survive) says (Example: "I can't")

• ways to get other people to take care of you (let you take care of them, do what you want, etc.)

• ways to be responsible to yourself

• ways to cop out

Whips

(Try small groups of 5, each group responding aloud to each task you write on the board, with the option to "pass" and *no discussion.*)

• I can . . .(Go at least 20 times around)

• I can't . . . (Afterwards, have them change these to "I won't . . .")

• I don't like me when I . . .

• I want to . . . (go 10 times around)

• A way I want to change myself is . . .

• I cop out when . . .

• I know that if I really decided to do it, I could . . .

• Something I haven't been totally honest with myself about concerns . . .

• I sometimes scare myself that . . .

Guided Fantasy

(Soft background music . . . eight second pause at each set of dots . . .)

The Wise Old Person

"Let your eyes close softly and focus attention on your breathing . . . forget about other people around you . . . relax your body . . . find any place with tension, and practice relaxing it . . . now, take a few deep breaths . . . and find yourself in a meadow . . . at the foot of a mountain. Your goal lies somehow at the top of that mountain, and you know you must go, but, just now, see the meadow . . . and hear the meadow . . . smell the meadow . . . touch the meadow . . . taste the meadow . . . now look around you once more, and bid goodbye to the meadow . . . and now, turn away, and begin to climb the mountain . . . I will give you some time to yourself. Now, to climb the mountain . . . (allow 1 1/2 minutes) . . . unless you are already at the top, and there you see a cave in the rocks, where dwells the wise old person you came to see . . . as you approach the cave, you see the wise old person sitting in it . . . now, you may ask this person any question you like; but, right now, think what question you will ask — because you only get one . . . ask the old person the question . . . hear the old person answer . . ."

(Continue the fantasy to include descending the mountain to the meadow, returning to the here and now, etc. After the fantasy, process with journals, sharing in partners or group, etc.)

VPR

"Close your eyes and see three figures, two at one side and one at the other . . . There is a drama (or game or script) unfolding here, and it concerns a Victim — notice which figure that is . . . and a Rescuer — notice which figure *that* is . . . and a Persecutor — notice which figure *that* is . . . now, see if you can see *which* one of the three figures . . . is *YOU!*"

Taking Responsibility

Big Me and Little Me

Following lead-up exercises (relaxation, etc.), ask group to imagine that there are two sets of glasses before them. One is a set belonging to Little Me.("Little Me is the little dancer in you, the part of you that is always afraid, always on the lookout for danger, always playing one part and acting the act, so you won't be hurt.") The other pair of glasses belongs to Big Me. ("Big Me is the wise old part of you that watches all the time, and sees, and knows better than to be afraid. Big Me is the part of you that is responsible, and that takes charge.") Give the group time to "look through" one pair of glasses, and then the other, at situations you structure, such as . . .

 __ someone who takes care of you
 __ a decision you have to make
 __ school
 __ someone you like
 __ someone you don't like
 __ a "scary" thing

Make up guided fantasies — or have children make them — entitled . . .

 — The Reward for Being Honest with Myself
 — Moving Up One Notch on the Responsibility Scale
 — Coming Clean with Someone
 — Big Me and Money (work, sex, parents, relationships, school, career, TV, food, religion, etc.)
 — Getting Taken Care Of

Activities

☆

Diad Roleplays.

Stand or seat people as partners, facing each other. Have each diad (a) act out a roleplay as you announce it (one person simply starts playing one of the roles); (b) reverse roles as you give another signal; (c) talk about (process) the feelings felt in each role; and (d) switch partners for the next roleplay assignment. Counting all four steps, about 5 minutes is the required time in any diad.

Suggestions for roleplay assignments:

> You've Got It and I Want It
> Victim and Good Samaritan
> Naughty Kid and Nice Kid
> Blamer and Blamee
> Solution-Suggester and Yeh-But-er
> Do-Gooder and Fake Victim
> Do-Gooder and Loner-Who-Doesn't-Want-To-Be-Rescued
> Big-Me and Little-Me
> Puppet and Wise Old Owl

Sit facing a partner. Maintain eye contact, no talking. Each of you now think of a specific *decision you are making,* or will have to make. Take turns asking each other the following questions, and pausing so that the person can apply the question to the area of decision:

Questions to ask in diads (without telling what issues are brought up)

> What *can't* you do about it?
> What *haven't* you done about it?
> What *must* you do about it?
> What do you *want* to do about it?
> What *have* you done about it?

Taking Responsibility

What *should* you do about it?
What *will* you do about it?

Process by asking:

In each case, what ego state (Big-Me or Little-Me) were you answering from?

What questions did you make yourself uncomfortable with?
What questions were you most comfortable with?
What questions elicited more *energy* in your response?

For Journal Writing:

What was doing this exercise like for you? Why?

What aspects of your decision are clearer to you now?

☆

Bumper Stickers and Campaign Buttons

Have students work in groups of three to brainstorm (and manufacture) bumper stickers and/or buttons with messages that promote self-responsibility. Examples:

YES, YOU CAN
SO WHAT?
YOU DO YOU AND I'LL DO ME

☆

Repeated Questions

Form partners, facing. Designate who's A and who's B. A asks B the same question, again and again, and B gives alternate answers. After 2 minutes, reverse roles. Process briefly, and move to new partner for a new question assignment.

Questions:

> What can you do?
> What won't you do?
> Who are you?
> What do you want?
> When do you cop out?
> What are you afraid of?
> What will you attempt?
> When do you pretend?
> What are you sure of?
> What do you forget to remember?
> Who aren't you responsible for?

☆

Big Me and Little Me

It is amazing, how this construct of the self can be grasped, by people young or old, and utilized in talk. Once these parts of us or "ego states" are defined, they can become part of everyday classroom language —

Examples:

> "When you say that, is that Big Me or Little Me?"

> "My Little Me wants to cry 'unfair!' right now — and my Big Me is just letting you know how Little Me feels, without fuss."

Use of Big Me and Little Me in classroom lingo focuses responsibility. To reinforce the concept have groups create illustrations of Big Me and Little Me in the form of bulletin boards, comic strips, skits and plays or other art forms. Whenever appropriate, play your part in self-disclosure, *model*ing, assuming responsibility through letting students know which part of you is talking — and which part of each of them you are hearing, etc.

Anti-Rescue League

Start an ARL, designed to "help-stamp-out-doing-for-others-what-they-can-do-for-themselves." Some ideas:

- Create a wall-size sign: SO WHAT?

- Make campaign buttons with the "international symbol" of or else saying anti-rescue statements like

  — "I can be responsible — and so can you!"

  — "Yes, you can"

  — "Misery is optional"

  — "Notice that you choose"

  — "So?"

- A "peaceful demonstration march" in favor of student self-responsibility

- A "fight corner" where kids work out their own disagreements without asking the teacher to handle it

- Beginning of teacher-class shared planning, decision-making and evaluation of limited portions of the curriculum

Where Opposites Connect

Introduction

It is often stated that western man in his technological hurry to build his body of logical knowledge, has tended to divide the universe into pieces and thus has dimished his own capacity to appreciate the essential oneness of it, and his part in that oneness. (In the West, we have stressed the "Yang" — or creative, assertive force — and acted almost as if there were no "Yin" — mysterious, destructive — to compliment it. Thus, we have lost the "balance," the sense of the essential "all-rightness" of things.) Either-or thinking, a moderately useful tool at this stage of our development, is of almost no use at all when it comes to *relating* — to self, others, or environment. A bi-polar mentality, imposed upon human relations, is the seat of what we have come to call "first impressions," "prejudices," "stereotypes," etc. associated with the -isms. In fact, the world is put-together, and every piece belongs. It is only our *way of seeing*, that takes it all apart. Our eyes (both physical and "inner" or intuitive seeing) can be taught to see, at any time, what is really going on, by integrating any event with its context. Either-or thinking (stereotypic, isolative) can be changed to both — and thinking (integrative, creative), with no threat to the seer except the loss of a blind spot. Actually, "opposites" are only labels, not things themselves. Nothing is like any other thing, yet everything is like everything else. Any two events can be seen actually to be connected to each other in myriad ways, for "any event creates the universe." This unit is designed to help students bring integrative or holistic thinking to bear upon solution-finding in their own lives.

Purposes

* To teach "spectrum thinking" — a kind a perceiving that stresses the relatedness of the thing observed to all other things

* To cause students to recognize and re-examine their own labels, stereotypes and prejudices

* To help students experience themselves more at home in an environment where "all things belong" by experiencing their own *acceptance*

* To train students to assume *relatedness* (not sameness) in others and themselves; and thus to bring a set of *belongingness* (rather than alienation) to the perception of all events.

Definition

1. Brainstorm a long list of opposites (up and down, on and off, truth and falsehood, etc.). A good way to do this is to have each student write an individual list of 10 items, then call out items while you construct a "master list" on newsprint; ask for unused items until eveyone's items are covered in the latter list. (This is a good occasional substitute for the oral group brainstorm, for it gives time for thought, eliminates crowding, validates and includes each participant.)

2. Now have each student code its original list of ten thusly: circle the word in each set of opposites that represents the end with which you identify most (i.e. good - evil, in - out).
Class now forms pairs: and walk thru the following alternating working alone and working with a partner

3. Choose one set of opposites ("one that has particular meaning for you both") from the master list with which to create a spectrum. On each end of a strip of paper 3" x 12" is ideal, write one of the two "opposites" — mark the midpoint and assign a word to it that represents a midpoint value. Then, create "one-quarter" points on the spectrum and do the same:

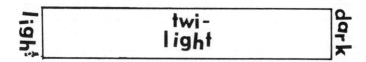

Notice that there are literally an infinite number of "value points" on the spectrum on which these "opposites" represent endpoints. "Now, relax and close your eyes. Forget where you are and what you've been doing . . . For one minute, imagine an event or issue in your current life that represents a *problem* or *concern* for you — "something you have mixed feelings about." Try to actually *see* or *symbolize* in an "awake dream" what that issue is or is about for you. (Allow one minute for this).

Open your eyes, look at your spectrum strip, and imagine that it tells you about one aspect of the very issue you just dreamed about (or, more specifically, about you and that issue). At various points on the strip, draw symbols that stand for:

- you
- other(s) in the problem
- something in the problem about
  - ____ time
  - ____ power
  - ____ money, energy, or whatever is spent
  - ____ rules
  - ____ other (what?)

Bend the strip into a circle and connect the "opposite ends" with tape. Contemplate these constructions for 1 minute. "Empty your mind of thoughts . . . gaze at the construction and be open to *another way of seeing* that you possibly may use . . ." Ask: "As you let this model of the circle speak to you, what things did you notice?" Discuss in partners for two minutes; then open to a short group rap. (Avoid the notion of a "right answer" in the discussion. A student may say something like, "What looked like opposites to me actually come from the same place!" Another may state, "But that's not *right!* Opposites are opposites!" Make room for everyone's comments by reflecting each in turn . . . "You're seeing that opposites may have things in common," or "There's something here you don't *agree* with, somehow.")

Ask: "What can this circle model *tell* you about you, your problem, or the way you've been looking at it?"

Now or at another time, have students use this or another pair of opposites in constructing the Chinese Yin-Yang symbol and contemplate it for insights about "Connections between opposites."

(In either of the symbology exercises above, the entire list of ten opposites may be imposed on this or any problem.)

Where Opposites Connect

Using the spectrum model to illustrate dimensional field:

This lecture-demonstration is a key part of opening up the concept of "opposites" to include relatedness. Use it early in the unit . .

1. Have someone think of a pair of opposites (say, "happy and sad"), and write them at opposite ends of the chalkboard.

2. Say, "sometimes when we think of things as opposites, we divide them in our minds so much that we forget that they are *related* (draw a line connecting the words) in many other ways. For instance, these are both emotions."

3. "Now, find me a word for a point *here* (place an X at the midpoint). Note now that we have a *relationship* between these opposites — a line or field in which many other points lie. Name several others. (As students name a feeling-word that lies in the happy-sad dimension, have them each come up and place it appropriately on the diagram. Note that some extremes like "euphoric" or "depressed" might lie outside the so-called opposites.)

4. Ask: "How can we express the *relationship* without which these words or ideas would not be "opposites?" Let's call it a *dimension* (or spectrum, line, field, continuum, etc. Decide on a name you can use together with comfort and consensus.)

Discussion Starters

• Use the brainstorm of opposites list for this. Students pair up, and each pair selects a set of opposites from the list. For 3 minutes each pair brainstorms all the ways those opposites are *like each other*. (*Example:* in and out: both are directions, both are English words, have *feelings* connected to them, etc. You may need to demonstrate with a quick class-size brainstorm at first.) Then, in rapid succession,

— Have partners take turns teaching each other for one minute the word in the pair of opposites they feel most positively about, and why.

— Switch partners, and have pairs select a new pair of opposites. For 2 minutes, each "becomes" one of the opposites, and talks with the other from that role, using "I." Exchange roles after one minute.

— Switch partners. For three minutes, discuss one pair of opposites selected from the standpoint of how each "needs" the other, as its "un-thing," for its own essence. "Give examples from your own experience."

• Labels: What are the most commonly used "opposite" words? (Good and bad, right and wrong, etc.) Note that these are not things, but *labels* for things. These labels tell more about *us* than about the things (events) we use them on. They tell us how we *feel* about the events.

• We are a team of wordsmiths, constructing a dictionary from scratch? What *are* opposites? Can we arrive at a definition we can all buy?

• Place on board:

1. up and down
2. good and bad
3. salt and pepper
4. add and subtract
5. wet and dry
6. hot and cold

Ask: Which of these is *not* a set of opposites? Why? (In the discussion, establish that set 3, salt and pepper, is the only set that does not arrange itself along an easy *continuum*, i.e. in set 1, "(vertical) direction." What is a name we could give to each other set's continuum? (If it is argued, for set 3, that "taste" is the continuum, ask what the midpoint of such a continuum would be called.)

Keep this academic phase of the discussion as brief as possible, in order to lead, with consensus and continuity, into the following:

__ Divide into 2's for brainstorming with no recording:

   A asks B: "What is your opposite?"
   B (a girl) answers, for example, "a boy"
   A asks again: "What is your opposite?"
   B gives a different response each time.

   Switch roles after two minutes. Coach askers to ask the question the same way each time.

   Process in large or support groups (small groups of 5 to 8 students who meet periodically for support tasks. See volume 2 of *Strategies* for description.)

__ How did it feel to be asked, again and again, the same question? What did you experience as the asker?

__ Share insights about the behavior of the group itself, doing this exercise — the what-I-notice-right-here-now-about-*us* and what is implied telepathically (though possibly unconsciously)

__ Which "opposite" named by each in the exercise above "sticks out" to that person as having emotional voltage? "Which opposite did you have (good or bad) feelings about? (Partners identify these items.)

"Each of you now, relax, close your eyes, let go of things we've been doing here, and things around you, for a moment . . .

Just now far, far away from off in the distance see . . . that *opposite* you just told yourself about when your partner was there . . . see what it is . . . see that it *is* that opposite you told yourself about . . . see it in detail . . . but notice that it is far off, a great distance from you . . . gaze at it awhile without thinking . . . just, watch it . . . now, slowly begin to bring it nearer to you, so that you can see it better . . . notice now, as it sloooo-wly approaches . . . that you are seeing things about it you didn't notice just a moment ago . . . keep *noticing new things* about that object . . . bring it close enough to touch . . . and now, reach out and experience what it *feels* like . . . just now, finish feeling around on it, and have it go farther away . . . slowly, farther and farther away . . . and slowly, until it is beginning to be difficult to see it again . . . and you watch it . . . disappear . . .

Processing: Students may tell themselves (via journal entry or meditation time), or others (partners, small or large group) about their experiences in the fantasy — or illustrate it or share in some other way.

Circletime

Note: To the usual Circletime format of recognition by reflection of feelings, add this task: Identify the name of the dimension or spectrum along which these "opposites" are arranged (i.e. "My friend and I are opposite in the dimension of being alone, etc.")

• A strong 'opposite' of mine

• What usually happens when I oppose (am opposed)

• Personality opposites' I've observed

- Someone (Not by name or I.D.) who feels like my 'opposite'

- The exact opposite kind of day (friend, parent, teacher, job, mate, etc.) I'd like to have

Journal Entries

- Relationship Symbols: Think of a person you are "opposite" of (some distance from on a specific dimension), and name what that dimension is. (Example: you feel far from someone because they get their needs met in a very different way than you.) Draw a map or picture or symbol of some sort an illustration that demonstrates how you and this other person are very *close* to one another in at least two other dimensions (example: height). How will you "map out" this illustration?

- Make three columns, numbered 1 to 10. In the first, list ten of your favorite things to do. In column 1, next to each item in column 1, write the exact *opposite* of each. In column 3, name the *dimension* along which your favorite and its "opposite" are placed (i.e., what they are opposites "in").

- Write a name that represents an "opposite" of some kind for you. Now, next to the name, list some words about that person, behavior or other item that is your "opposite." Now, reflect on each item on the list, using the notion "The opposite of _____ is me . . ." Check with your feelings in each case. Along what *other* dimension might the "opposite" thing be closer to your favorite item?

Activities

☆

Show the film "Where All Things Belong," available from Essentia, P.O. Box 129 Tiburon, CA. 94920

☆

Experiencing the Opposite

Think of something you do, something simple or routine. Now, think of its "opposite" — a behavior that seems opposite, like tying your shoelaces backwards, or folding your arms in reverse. (Choose something you do repeatedly in a day.) Name the dimension along which you see these as opposites.

Spend an entire day doing the "opposite" of what you usually do.

☆

Opposites to Me

Below, write the names of 3 "opposites" of yours from the class group, and the dimensions along which each is "opposite":

_____ is opposite to me in _____

Next, for each of the three, list three other dimensions along which that person and you are *close* to one another. (*Example:* Ann is opposite to me in physical strength but close to me in hair color and temperment.)

☆

Now or at some other time, have students create "Yin-Yang" symbols with their spectrum strips (or ones made from another pair of opposites) bending the strip (A) between the sides of another longer strip (B).

Next, trace the designs on paper (fig. I on white paper and fig. II on black paper). Cut them out, (place an "eye" (E) of the opposing color on each figure) and fit the figure together.

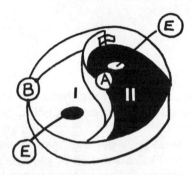

This time, explain that work with the figures will be mostly alone, and without talking. With the constructions in front of them, students contemplate the continuous with respect to their problems. Journals should be handy, for noting down anything of an "aha" or "I see" nature.

In the large group discussion following some sharing of insights or other reactions to the exercise, push for more contributions of a 'so-what?' nature.

Roleplays

- Opposites: Brainstorm a list of "opposite" roles (i.e. good kid, bad kid, smart-dumb, etc.) Divide class into pairs, who sit facing each other for 2 minute roleplays (changing roles at the one minute signal); then stop and talk about the acitivty for 1 minute in pairs, then share at large in the group. Switch partners with a nearby pair, and start a new roleplay round.

- Have small groups:

  1. Choose a kind of *behavior* as a dimension, and create a six-point continuum (see Volume I of *Strategies*), showing endpoints and four interval points.

  2. Have the group prepare and present the continuum by acting it out.

Example:　　　*Behavior: "Telling about bad breath"*

1.	2.	3.	4.	5.
suffering in silence	keeping a distance	clearing throat a lot, asking if person needs time out to "freshen up" etc.	embarassedly presenting the person with mouthwash	confronting the person deliberately, with request to brush teeth, chew gum, get new breath

- Caricatures: Have groups of three prepare and present short skits in which they play caricatures of their "opposite selves" (i.e. if one is very calm and cool, this one plays him/herself as nervous and flighty, etc.)

- Group Continuums: This is best done in groups of about 8-10. Assign two students in each group to collaborate on a set of "opposites" to act out (*Example:* pleasure — pain)These two stand some distance apart and begin their replay — which may be more of a pantomine. Other group members are to arrange themselves along an imaginary contiuum (the line between the "opposites"), and act out the roles their positions imply.

Brainstorms

- Items that would arrange (not in any order) along a spectrum of . . .

  — excellent to awful (i.e. "good," "bad," "promising," "Incapable," "worse," etc.)

  — bully to "rescuer"

  — angel to devil

  — all to nothing

  — what else?

  If you record these, code the lists by number to arrange in the order of the spectrum.)

- For one minute, brainstorm and record things that begin with B . . . Now, label each item with an O if it has what could be considered an opposite. (*Example*: "Bear" has no opposite, but "boring" has "entertaining.") List the O - items separately. Next to each, determine its opposite, and the dimension on which those items arrange.

- Being Shot Thru with Dimensions: Minimum of thirty; items:

  On how many different dimensions are we all, just this moment, arranging ourselves? (Example: talk-listen, tall-short, high energy-low energy, etc.)

- Subtitles: In groups of 5, for two minutes, call out all the minorities of which each of you is a member. (Example: people with red socks on, over 10 years old, females, Americans, birthday in March, etc.)

  Process: How does it feel to belong to that many groups? (Enlarge to: when we focus on our connectedness to all that is, we're often strangely euphoric.)

- Feelings Brainstorm: Brainstorm a list of feelings (about 30). Next, write an "opposite" feeling for each item.

- Flipside: Explain that, because these feelings can all come from the same person as origin, and since apparently opposed strong feelings of both a positive and a negative nature are ofter *experienced* in similar ways, it is safe to pretend as if they come from the same creative force inside a person, and thus to say that one is simply "the other side" of the other. Have students break up into 3's and discuss (general rap for 10 minutes, with strong hints to keep *personal* — "say" "I" and relate what you are saying to your own experience."):

Task: Choose an item and its opposite from the feelings brainstorm. (Example: "sadness-happiness.") Insert it in the sentence: _____ is the other side _____." (Example: "*Sadness* is the other side of *happiness*.") Now, give an example from your own feelings that might support the statement. (Example: "I cry both times.")

Appendix

(Reprint of strategies from Volume 1 and 2)

Forced Choice

The forced choice strategy affords opportunities for youngsters to *make decisions* regarding their own values, behaviors and view of the world. There is no qualifying with a forced choice exercise (except that you can offer chances to have students explain or qualify their responses, or you can, if you wish, create a "can't decide" category). Often it's helpful to introduce a forced choice by saying . . .

If you had to be one or the other, would you be . . . ?

If you *had* to do one or the other, would you . . . ?

If you *could only do one,* would you . . . ?

Forced choice activities can be conducted publicly (with a partner, small group, or total class with whom to share) or on paper (in journals or on scrap) or both.

Encourage the class to help you create new ones; varieties are endless. Criteria for creating forced choices:

•   keep number of choices small (2-5).

•   Try to give each choice equal "weight" with the others, to make the choice more "forced."

•   Vary the methods used (sometimes giving opportunity to explain or qualify, sometimes not; sometimes allowing sharing, other times having the responses be "Private office"; etc.)

Rank-Order

More choice-making practice! The Rank-Ordering strategy combines the essentials of Continuum and Forced Choice, in that it requires youngsters to make decisions regarding preferences, and to arrange those preferences along a continuum, from "most desirable" to "least desirable."

Often, when introducing this activity, after presenting the items it is helpful to say "Think: if you could have only *one* of these items, which would it be? (Mark that with a 1.) Now, look at what's left; if you could have only one again, which would it be? (Mark that with a 2.) etc., etc." After a while, kids will know what you mean if you simply say, "Rank-order these items" and put the list on the board.

If the list contains more than 3 items (and even with 3), we recommend that you require participants to *record* their rank-ordering choices on paper, even on "scratch" — just so they can commit to them. (This is especially important before verbal sharing, as people influence one another's choices quite easily.) This recording can easily be done if you ask students merely to write the numbers (or letters) of items you place on the board.

a. Give *groups of five* 10 minutes to come to agreement as to how to rank-order the list (they can use any means to achieve consensus *except* the vote, which leaves some people out).

b. Place *"number stations"* (areas marked with as many numbers as choices) around the room. Read an item, and have people walk to the station that represents what number on their list they ranked that item.

c. *Ask aloud.* "How many ranked the character of Little John second?" (Raising of hands.) "Would you like to tell why?"

d. *Create new criteria.* Items can be rank-ordered from any angle: importance, value to self, value to the world, beauty, size, kookiness, longevity, contribution, despicableness, challenge, etc.

Continuum, (or spectrum)

"Continuum" represents not only a set of strategies, but a way of thinking or perceiving which has definite advantages in approaching a problem. The continuum exercises suggested in this book are thus to be considered in their broadest objective, as building a *mentality,* or a *thinking tool,* through much practice.

In a continuum model, we preceive an endless variety of possibilities. Continuum thinking is essentially *both / and* thinking (in contrast to *either / or* thinking). It is *in*clusive, instead of *ex*clusive. Thus, it is designed to open up, rather than limit, the realm of possibilities (Brainstorming is an example of continuum thinking.)

Some points to remember about using the continuum strategy:

1. *Always create radical or extreme or ridiculous endpoints.* Endpoints should be difficult for students to identify with.

2. *Encourage sharing.* Let volunteers tell the group *why* they are standing (or having their initials placed) where they are.

3. *Take your own turn.* Students need to know where you stand also.

Inventories

The inventory tells something to the reader about the kind of person s/he is or could be.

Each person is asked to list either as many things as they can think of, or to list a specific number of things. But this is only the first step. An inventory is more than the list.

The second step is to code the list in a way that helps the student to see some inclinations or create some awareness not held before.

As the students complete the coding they will be able to get a clearer picture of themselves. There will also be some things to decide on. Do they want to maintain their present behavior pattern? Do they see something that surprises them? Are they pleased/displeased with their inventory? You, as leader, can assist them in their process of self-awareness by asking these kinds of process questions.

Circletime*

A *circletime* is an activity which can be carried on with a group of children numbering from five to an entire class. It is designed primarily as a small-group experience; ideal-sized groups go from five (at levels pre-school through second grade) up to twelve (sixth grade and beyond). Usually seated in a circle, the teacher and children spend from ten to twenty minutes a session, communicating around a topic. Readily distinguishable from a discussion or rap session, circletime focuses each session on a new segment of common human experience. The major goals of a circletime are (a) to foster self-awareness in children, and (b) to build skills of effectively sharing and listening to feelings.

The rules of the circletime, repeated each session at the beginning, are:

- Everyone gets a turn who wants to.

- Everyone who takes a turn gets listened to.

These rules focus on the communications processes through which the activity builds skills of sharing and listening. The second rule, by example of the teacher and gradual involvement of the kids as the routine way of responding, becomes defined in practice as, "Everyone who shares gets *feedback*, on a here's-what-I-heard-you-say basis."

Following the review of rules, the teacher gives the task for the day and the interaction begins.

---

* This activity is much more fully covered as an entire year's curriculum of affective growth for each grade level, in our publication entitled *Circlebook*.

Interaction continues as long as people want turns, including the teacher. There is no questioning ("Was that at night or during the day?"), no commenting ("I know what you mean because I had an operation once . . ."), no directive responses at all. The reason (beyond mere time restriction) that responding modes are thus limited becomes clear when the *primary goal* of circletime — *building self-awareness* — is considered. In this model — a kind of "listening laboratory" for the world of feelings — it is the *speaker's* needs to be listened to that take priority. Therefore, responses are generally limited to *mirroring.*

Discussion Methods

A discussion can be an effective learning experience — or it can be a turnoff for kids. Many teachers teach largely by discussion, whereas others rarely use this tool in the classroom. Analysis of classroom interactions where much discussion takes place (i.e., where the teacher is comfortable with discussion as a teaching style) reveals that often the teacher is talking much more than the students — and does not know it.

Here are some suggestions to make discussion more engaging, effective and facilitative of learning for all kids:

1. *Start with a "discrepant event,"* such as a catchy sentence, a roleplay presentation a group has previously prepared, a picture, a behavior — something that calls attention in a slightly jarring way, something that "makes heads turn" a little. Letting something dynamic initiate a discussion builds far more motivation than "Now let's talk about . . ."

2. *Structure for quick, easy responses by everyone.* This can be done by placing an issue statement ("Reading is a better use of time than watching TV.") on the board and asking for one-sentence responses; or by using a sentence stem ("If I had a million dollars . . .") and having each student write out a response before sharing — or doing a "whip" by going around the class in order, having each child complete the sentence aloud or say "pass."

3. *Don't be afraid of silences,* be aware of who talks more — you or the kids. Practice economy of words yourself. Extend your own "wait time," both after your question, and (harder, but very effective) after a student's response to your question. Try to make your comments only the needed ones — be open-ended and facilitative. Model listening rather than talking. Give time to ponder and wonder. One way to do this is to lose eye-contact with the speaker. Look around the class when a student is talking; you will notice others paying more attention to the speaker than to you.

4. *No easy answer, or no one right answer.* You will involve more of the group if it is evident from the outset that all contributions will be encouraged and protected from judgement. Where there *is* only one right answer, use another technique for learning than discussion. A discussion should never be a public exercise for dividing winners from losers.

5. When the material under discussion lends itself to a dip into a more personal dimension, use such questions as:

   What would *you* have done?
   Has anything like this ever happened to *you*?

6. *Maintain a facilitator or moderator role.* Demonstrate your neutrality, encourage contributions by reflecting what kids say. Responses by you that clarify what contributors say are valued by all; they show respect and interest on your part. Sum up the ideas the group generates, using the chalkboard or a flipchart to record.

7. *Allow for non-closure.* Just because kids don't have "the answer," don't think learning and involvement aren't happening. Stop discussion when the group's *energy* peaks, *not* when the answer is reached.

8. *Process the discussion.* Deal with here-and-now thoughts, feelings and behaviors by occasionally stopping to ask things like:

   What does it feel like to do this?
   How do you feel now, that's different from when we started?
   What kinds of things do you find yourself thinking about here?
   Are we on or off the subject? How can we get back?
   What do we want to do with this, as a group?

Journals

Journals are usually ongoing classroom diaries of personal experience that may or may not be shared with the teacher and/or others. You can have children make and decorate their own, use ditto'd handouts that become pages in the journal, use notebook forms — whatever suits you. Periodically, allow ten to twenty minutes for students to write in their journals. You can use a variety of approaches to journals — for instance, having some entries drawn instead of written. There should be common understanding from the first about *what* is shared from journals and *how* it is shared. Because of the personal nature of this activity (sometimes children who rarely talk at all will write a great deal of revealing things in journals), you should respect and enforce what is decided regarding who reads journals.

If, as is common, the teacher periodically collects the journals for reading, be sure to write comments in all books — if not all entries — to show that you have read them. This can become an exhausting task, so limit it from the beginning, or be ready at any time to announce: "I need help! I can't respond to all the things you're writing." On the other hand, if children are sharing little of themselves, trust needs to be build; perhaps the sharing guidelines need revision. Basically, journals are for kids, not teachers. It is the self-awareness that comes through responding on paper to an affectively-oriented task that is the objective here.

Role Play

Guidelines for roleplays:

1. Be specific about who's who in the roleplay, but give little more in the way of background than role, age, name and sex of the person being portrayed.

2. Keep roleplays short (1 to 3 minutes).

3. Assign observers to watch for specific elements (evidences of emotion, tone, pace, body language, etc.), and not simply be entertained.

4. Vary format between practiced, performance-type roleplays, and unrehearsed roleplays (usually more ef- fective in terms of spontaneous, here-and-now learning).

5. After stopping the roleplay, allow the players to share their feelings first, then observers to tell what they saw or heard.

6. Process the roleplay both on a "what" and a "so-what" level. That is, deal both with what-we-saw-happening-here and how-this-is-like-in-real-life-situations. (See the section on processing skills for additional ways to deal with the roleplay after it is over.)

7. Always focus attention more on the *behaviors and feelings* generated during the roleplay, than on acting ability or specific outcomes.

Brainstorming

The rules of any brainstorm are simple. It is useful to post them and review them before beginning a brainstorm:

Do's

*   Make as long a list as you can.

*   Record everything.

*   Go far-out — nothing is too wild.

*   "Piggyback" (borrow on ideas).

Dont's

*   No right, no wrongs, no evaluations.

*   No discussing, questioning or defending any item.

Before presenting any of the activities under any one topic heading, first spend one or two days' sessions brainstorming the topic head as described below; then move into the activities under the heading and stay on that topic for awhile, as in the unit approach.

Brainstorm a definition.

Write the topic word or phrase on the board, with the word "is" after it (as in "Body is . . ."). Then ask the class to give *other* names for body. Show that you want not examples but definitions. Become the "scribe" for the class, and encourage them, through you as a writer, to fill up the board with other words for the topic. These need not be single words. In fact, once you have made the task clear, be entirely uncritical of what comes, and write it all down. If someone is off task, let the group police them back. Write everything down, but if other things than definitions are given (i.e., examples), write these off to one side. At the end, have the group tell why you wrote them separately.

Processing

What we are calling humanistic education could also rightly be called "process education," for it involves a continual looking at the "how" of human behavior. In school, there tends to be great emphasis on the "what," the stuff of learning. *How* something is learned may be (probably is) more important than the something itself. The processing techniques presented here attempt to make this awareness happen in the midst of, or immediately after, an experience.

This list of process questions will give you an idea of what interventions you can make in simple ways to raise children's consciousness of themselves and of others:

During the exercise:

• What is *going on* right now?

• How do you *feel* about what is happening?

• What was the last thought you just thought?

- Become aware of how your *body* feels right now.

- Where are we in terms of the *task*?

- What do you *want*?

- How can we get where we want to *go*?

- What does the group *need* right now?

- *If I said* _____ how would you feel? (Time for a break, stop, let's work thirty minutes more on this, you don't have to finish, etc.)

- If you were to *give a title* to what's happening, what would it be?

After the Exercise

- Respond on paper to any of these *sentence-stems* on the board that are appropriate to you:

    I learned _____ (to, that, that I, that others . . .)

    I was most comfortable about _____ .

    I was most uncomfortable about _____ .

    I wish _____ .

    I wonder _____ .

    I wanted more (less) _____ .

- Collect *"highs"* and *"lows"* from this activity.

- *Thumbs up.* (If children like the activity they hold thumbs up; if not, thumbs down. If neutral, make a fist. If feel strongly, circulate thumbs in air. All do this at once, and look around for an instant "fix" on group reaction.)

- *Journal entries.* Journals make excellent ongoing process records; have students write entries, using one or another of the methods here, after an activity from this book, or after a test or lesson from the content curriculum.

- *Yaa-boo.* Teacher names various aspects, or steps in the sequence of the activity, and students all whisper loudly either "yay" or "boo" according to how they feel about it.

Bibliography of Humanistic-Education Cookbooks

Each item on the following suggested reading list has been selected because of its eminent **usuability** by classroom teachers. We call this a list of "cookbooks" because, unlike theoretical treatises on why humanistic education is a good thing, books by visionaries about why schools have to change, etc., these are books of strategies, actual recipes for making changes in your classroom day to provide for affective development. By its appearance on this list, a book qualifies as a "cookbook" in that its material can be easily:

1. adapted into a philosophical education structure we call "humanistic education" (i.e. is consistent with the assumptions listed at the beginning of this book)
2. replicated in the classroom
3. adapted to age or grade level, or to particular group needs.

Ballard, Jim. **Stop A Moment: A Group Leader's Handbook of Energizing Experiences**, Amherst, Mass: Mandala, 1977.

Ballard, Jim. **Circlebook**, Mandala, 1975, Amherst, Mass.

Bates. **Better Eyesight Without Glasses**, Pyramid Books, 1970.

Bennett, H. and Samuels, M. **Be Well**, New York: Random House, 1975.

Bennett, H. and Samuels, M. **The Well Body Book**, New York: Random House, 1973.

Benson. **The Relaxation Response**, New York: Avon, 1976.

Berger, Terry. **I Have Feelings**, New York: Behavioral Publications. 1974.

Bernhard, Yetta. **How To Be Somebody: Open the Door to Personal Growth**, Millbrae, California: Celestial Arts, 1975.

Bessell, Harold and Palomares, Uvaldo. **Methods in Human Development-Theory Manual**, San Diego, California: Human Development Training Institute, 1973.

Borton, Terry. **Reach, Touch and Teach**, New York, McGraw-Hill Book Company, 1970.

Brayer, Herbert O. and Cleary, Zella W. **Valuing in the Family: A Workshop Guide for Parents**, San Diego, California: Pennant Press, 1972.

Brown, George Isaac. **Human Teaching for Human Learning — An Introduction to Confluent Education**, New York: The Viking Press, 1971.

Brown, George Isaac. **The Live Classroom**, New York: The Viking Press, 1975.

Canfield, John and Wells, Harold. **100 Ways to Enhance Self-Concept in the Classroom**, Englewood Cliffs, N.J.: Prentice-Hall, Inc. 1975.

Cassel, Pearl and Dreikurs, Rudolf. **Discipline Without Tears**, New York: Hawthorn Books, Inc., 1972.

Charles, Cheryl I and Stadsklev, Ronald. **Learning With Games**, An Analysis of Social Studies Educational Games and Simulations, Boulder, Colorado: The Social Science Education Consortium, Inc. 1973.

Chase, Larry, **The Other Side of the Report Card**, Goodyear Pub., Pacific Palisades, Calif. 1975.

Cullum, Albert. **Push Back the Desks**, British Commonwealth: Harlin Quist, Inc. 1967.

DeMille, Richard. **Put Your Mother on the Ceiling**, Walker and Co. N.Y. 1967.

Dreikurs, Rudolf. **Coping With Children's Misbehavior**: A Parent's Guide, New York: Hawthorn Books, Inc., 1972.

Earnst, Ken. **Games Students Play** (And What To Do About Them), Millbrae, California: Celestial Arts Publishing, 1972.

Fadiman, James and Hendricks Gay, Ed. **Transpersonal Education: A Curriculum for Feeling and Being**: Englewood Cliffs, N.J.: Prentice-Hall, 1976.

Fluegelman, Andrew, Ed. **The New Game Book**, Garden City, New York: A Headlands Press Book (a division of Doubleday and Co., Inc.), 1976.

Furness, Pauline. **Role-Play in the Elementary School: A Handbook for Teachers**, New York City: Hart Publishing Co., 1976.

Galbraith, Ronald E. and Jones, Thomas M. **Moral Reasoning: A Teaching Handbook for Adapting Kohlberg to the Classroom**, Minneapolis, Minnesota: Greenhaven Press Inc., 1976.

Ginott, Haim. **Teacher and Child**, New York: The Macmillan Company, 1972.

Gordon, Thomas. **Parent Effectiveness Training**, New York: Peter H. Wyden, 1970.

-------**Teacher Effectiveness Training**, New York: Peter H. Wyden, 1974.

Gorman, Alfred H. **Teacher and Learners — The Interactive Process of Education**, Boston, Mass.: Allyn and Bacon, Inc., 1969.

Greer, Mary and Rubinstein, Bonnie. **Will the Real Teacher Please Stand Up?**, Pacific Palisades, California: Goodyear Publishing Company, 1972.

Gross, Beatrice and Ronald, Ed., **Will It Grow In a Classroom?** Delta Pub., N.Y. 1974.

Hawley, Robert and Hawley, Isabel. **Developing Human Potential**, Amherst Ma.: Education Research Associates. 1975.

Hawley, Robert and Hawley, Isabel, **Developing Human Potential**, Vol. 2, Amherst Ma., Education Research Associates, 1977.

Hawley Robert C. **Human Values in the Classroom**, Amherst Massachusetts: Education Research Associates, 1974.

Hawley, Robert C. and Isabel I. **A Handbook of Personal Growth Activities for Classroom Use**, Amherst, Massachusetts: Edcuation Research Associates, 1972.

Henderson. **The Long-Run Solution**, World Publishers, 1976.

Hendricks, G. and Roberts, T. **Centering Book**, Englewood Cliffs, New Jersey: Prentice-Hall, 1976.

Hendricks, G. and Roberts, T. **Second Centering Book**, Englewood Cliffs, New Jersey: Prentice-Hall, 1977.

Howe, Leland W. and Howe, Mary Martha. **Personalizing Education: Values Clarification and Beyond**, New York City: Hart Publishing Co., 1975.

James, Muriel and Jongeward, Dorothy. **Born to Win**, Reading Mass.: Addison-Wesley Publishing Company, 1971.

Johnson, David. **Reaching Out**, Englewood Cliffs, N.J.: Prentice-Hall, Inc., 1972.

Kostrubala, T. **The Joy of Running**, Lippincott, 1976.

Lewis, Howard and Streitfeld, Harold. **Growth Games**, N.Y. Harcourt Brace Jovanovich, Inc. 1970.

Maid, Amy and Timmermann, Tim. **Something for 10:30: Involvement Cards for Social Skills**, Amherst, Mass.: Mandala, 1978.

Masters. **How Your Mind Can Keep You Well**, New York: Fawcett Books, 1977.

Morrison, Eleanor and Mila Underhill Price. **Values in Sexuality**, N.Y.: Hart Publishing Co. Inc. 1974.

Ornstein R. **The Psychology of Consciousness**, Penguin, 1975.

Osborn, Alex F. **Applied Imagination**, Chas. Scribners' Sons, N.Y. 1963.

Pearce, Joseph Chilton. **The Crack in the Cosmic Egg**, The Julian Press, 1971.

Porat, Frieda. **Positive Selfishness**, Millbrae, California: Celestial Arts, 1977.

Raths, Louis, Harmin Merrill and Simon Sidney B., **Values in Teaching**, Columbus, Ohio, Charles E. Merrill, 1966.

Read, Donald S. and Simon Sidney B. (eds.), **Humanistic Education Sourcebook**, Englewood Cliffs, N.J., Prentice-Hall, Inc., 1975.

Reicher, Richard. **Self-Awareness Through Group Dynamics**, Dayton, Ohio: Pflaum/Standard, 1970.

Roberts, I. **The Nature of Personal Reality**, Englewood Cliffs, N.J.: Prentice Hall, 1974.

Sax, Saville and Hollander, Sandra. **Reality Games**, New York: Popular Library, 1972.

Schrank, Jeffrey. **Teaching Human Beings, 101 Subversive Activities for the Classroom**, Beacon Press, Boston 1972.

Simon, Sidney B., **Meeting Yourself Halfway**, Niles, Illinois, Argus Communications, 1974.

Simon, Sidney, et al,. **Values Clarification**, N.Y.: Hart Publishing Co., Inc., 1972.

Smith, A. **Powers of Mind**, New York: Random House, 1975.

Smith, Gerald. **Hidden Meanings**, Millbrae, California: Celestial **Arts, 1975.**

Stanford, Gene. Developing Effective Classroom Groups: A Practical Guide For Teachers, New York City: Hart Publishing Co., 1977.

Stevens, John. **Awareness**, Moab, Utah: Real People Press, 1971.

Thomas, Marlo. **Free to Be . . . You and Me**, New York: Webster Division, McGraw-Hill Book Company, 1974.

Timmermann, Tim. **Growing Up Alive**, Mandala, Amherst, Mass. 1975.

Weinstein, Gerald and Fantini, Mario D. **Toward Humanistic Education — A Curriculum of Affect**, New York: Praeger Publishers, 1972.

Wells, Harold C., **About Me**, Rosemont, Illinois: Combined Motivation Education Systems, Inc., 1970.

Wood, Jane. **Gimme Something To Feel**, Baltimore, Maryland: Penguin Books, 1973.

ABOUT YOU

Because this book is about *practice* — the business of doing
things with kids that are growthful, dynamic, and perhaps a bit
risky — we want you to consider yourself a kind of author of it.
Inasmuch as you try the things suggested here, bend them and
change them and experiment with them, you are writing this
curriculum in your own unique way. If you did not care about
the kind of things this book is about, you would probably not
have gotten involved with it enough with it to be reading this.
But because you *do* care, because children's growth in
awareness, feelings, behaviors, attitudes and developing values
do matter to you, we wish to congratulate you on what you're
doing, and on the kind of educator you are. Just in case no one
is giving you the recognition you deserve, take it from us:
You're very special, and you deserve a big hand!